Speaking of Silence in Heidegger

Speaking of Silence in Heidegger

Wanda Torres Gregory

LEXINGTON BOOKS
Lanham • Boulder • New York • London

Published by Lexington Books
An imprint of The Rowman & Littlefield Publishing Group, Inc.
4501 Forbes Boulevard, Suite 200, Lanham, Maryland 20706
www.rowman.com

86-90 Paul Street, London EC2A 4NE

British Library Cataloging in Publication Information Available

Library of Congress Cataloging-in-Publication Data

Names: Gregory, Wanda Torres, author.
Title: Speaking of silence in Heidegger / Wanda Torres Gregory.
Description: Lanham : Lexington Books, [2021] | Includes bibliographical references and index.
Identifiers: LCCN 2021034394 (print) | LCCN 2021034395 (ebook) | ISBN 9781793640031 (cloth) | ISBN 9781793640048 (ebook)
Subjects: LCSH: Heidegger, Martin, 1889-1976. | Silence (Philosophy) | Truth.
Classification: LCC B3279.H49 G7156 2021 (print) | LCC B3279.H49 (ebook) | DDC 193—dc23
LC record available at https://lccn.loc.gov/2021034394
LC ebook record available at https://lccn.loc.gov/2021034395

Contents

Acknowledgments

I would like to express my appreciation to my fellow Heidegger scholars for their encouraging feedback on earlier versions of portions of this book that were presented at the North Texas Heidegger Symposium, McKinney, Texas, April 21–22, 2017, and were accepted for presentations (canceled due to the pandemic) at the APA Pacific Conference, San Francisco, April 8–11, 2020, and the 54th Annual Heidegger Circle Meeting, Gonzaga University, Washington, May 14–17, 2020. I would also like to thank my anonymous reviewer for their constructive critiques. My gratitude goes to the Lexington Books team for their efficiency in making this book a reality. I am grateful to Simmons University as well for granting me a sabbatical in the fall of 2019 that enabled me to advance in my research and writing. Finally, my heartfelt thanks to my family and friends for their support, and especially to my friend, Dr. Donna Giancola, for being an authentic interlocutor in our conversations on silence.

Abbreviations

In my references to Heidegger's writings, the pagination of the original German text follows the quoted English pagination with a forward slash.

MARTIN HEIDEGGER, *GESAMTAUSGABE* (FRANKFURT: KLOSTERMANN, 1975–.)

GA5	*Holzwege* (1980). Dispersed translations (see Bibliography).
GA7	*Vorträge und Aufsätze* (2000). Dispersed translations (see Bibliography).
GA8	*Was Heisst Denken?* (2002). Translation: *What Is Called Thinking?,* trans. J. Glenn Gray (New York: Harper and Row, 1968).
GA9	*Wegmarken* (1976). Translation: *Pathmarks*, ed. William McNeill (Cambridge: Cambridge University Press, 1998).
GA13	*Aus der Erfahrung des Denkens* (2002).
GA15	*Seminare. Heraklit* (2014). Translation: *Heraclitus Seminar*, trans. Charles H. Seiber (Evanston: Northwestern University Press, 1994).
GA29/30	*Die Grundbegriffe der Metaphysik: Welt, Endlichkeit, Einsamkeit* (1983). Translation: *The Fundamental Concepts of Metaphysics: World, Finitude, Solitude*, trans. William McNeill and Nicholas Walker (Bloomington and Indianapolis: Indiana University Press, 1995).

GA34 *Vom Wesen der Wahrheit. Zu Platons Höhlengleichnis und* Theätet (1997). Translation: *On the Essence of Truth. On Plato's Cave Allegory and* Theatetus, trans. Ted Sadler (New York; London: Continuum, 2002).

GA36/37 *Sein und Wahrheit. 1. Die Grundfrage der Philosophie. 2. Vom Wesen der Wahrheit.* (2001). Translation: *Being and Truth*, trans. Gregory Fried and Richard Polt (Bloomington and Indianapolis: Indiana University Press, 2010).

GA38 *Logik als die Frage nach dem Wesen der Sprache* (1998). Translation: *Logic as the Question Concerning the Essence of Language*, trans. Wanda Torres Gregory and Yvonne Unna (Albany, New York: State University of New York Press, 2009).

GA39 *Hölderlins Hymnen "Germanien" und "Der Rhein"* (1989). Translation: *Hölderlin's Hymns "Germania" and "The Rhein,"* trans. William McNeill and Julia Anne Ireland (Indiana: Indiana University Press, 2014).

GA55 *Heraklit. Der Angang des abendländischen Denkens. Logik: Heraklits Lehre vom Logos* (1994). Translation: *Heraclitus. The Inception of Occidental Thinking and Logic: Heraclitus's Doctrine of the* Logos, trans. Julia Goesser Assaiante and S. Montgomery Ewegen (London: Bloomsbury Academic, 2018).

GA65 *Beiträge zur Philosophie (Vom Ereignis)* (1989). Translation: *Contributions to Philosophy (Of the Event),* trans. Richard Rojcewicz and Daniela Vallega-Neu (Bloomington and Indianapolis: Indiana University Press, 2012).

GA69 *Die Geschichte des Seyns* (1998; 2012). Translation: *The History of Beyng*, trans. William McNeill and Jeffrey Powell (Bloomington: Indiana University Press, 2015).

GA71 *Das Ereignis* (2009). Translation: *The Event*, trans. Richard Rojcewicz (Bloomington and Indianapolis: Indiana University Press, 2013).

GA74 *Zum Wesen der Sprache und Zur Frage nach der Kunst* (2011).

GA77 *Feldweg-Gespräche* (2007). Translation: *Country Path Conversations*, trans. Bret Davis (Bloomington: Indiana University Press, 2010).

GA79 *Bremer und Freiburger Vorträge. 1. Einblick in das was ist. 2. Grundsätze des Denken* (1994). Translation:

	Bremen and Freiburg Lectures. Insight into That Which Is and Basic Principles of Thinking, trans. Andrew J. Mitchell (Bloomington: Indiana University Press, 2012).
GA85	*Vom Wesen der Sprache. Die Metaphysik der Sprache und die Wesung des Wortes. Zu Herders Abhandlung "Über den Ursprung der Sprache"* (1999). Translation: *On the Essence of Language. The Metaphysics of Language and the Essencing of the Word. Concerning Herder's* Treatise on the Origin of Language, trans. Wanda Torres Gregory and Yvonne Unna (Albany, New York: State University of New York Press, 2004).
GA94 II–VI	*Überlegungen II–VI (Schwarze Hefte 1931–1938)* (2014). Translation: *Ponderings II–VI: Black Notebooks 1931–1938*, trans. Richard Rojcewicz (Bloomington and Indianapolis: Indiana University Press, 2016).
GA94 VII–XII	*Überlegungen VII–XII (Schwarze Hefte 1938–1939)* (2014). Translation: *Ponderings VII–XII: Black Notebooks 1938–1939,* trans. Richard Rojcewicz (Bloomington and Indianapolis: Indiana University Press, 2017).
GA94 XII–XV	*Überlegungen XII–XV (Schwarze Hefte 1939–1941)* (2014). Translation: *Ponderings XII–XV: Black Notebooks* 1939–1941, trans. Richard Rojcewicz (Bloomington and Indianapolis: Indiana University Press, 2017).

OTHER TEXTS BY HEIDEGGER

GE	*Gelassenheit* (Pfullingen: Neske, 1959). Translation: *Discourse on Thinking*, trans. John M. Anderson and E. Hans Freund (New York: Harper & Row, 1966).
HH	*Hebel-der Hausfreund* (Pfullingen: Neske, 1957). Translation: "Hebel-Friend of the House," *Contemporary German Philosophy* 3(1983): 89–101, trans. B.V. Flotz and M. Heim.
SG	*Der Satz vom Grund* (Stuttgart: Neske, 1997). Translation: *The Principle of Reason*, trans. Reginald Lilly (Bloomington and Indianapolis: Indiana University Press, 1996).
SZ	*Sein und Zeit* (Tübingen: Niemeyer, 1986). Translation: *Being and Time*, trans. John Macquarrie and Edward Robinson (New York: Harper and Row, 1962).

US	*Unterwegs zur Sprache* (Stuttgart: Neske, 1982). Translation: *On the Way to Language*, trans. Peter D. Hertz (New York: Harper & Row, 1971). The translation of "Sprache" as "Language" appears in *Poetry, Language, Thought*, trans. Albert Hofstadter (New York: Harper & Row, 1971).
UT	*Überlieferte Sprache und Technische Sprache* (St. Gallen: Erker, 1989). Translation: "Traditional Language and Technological Language," trans. Wanda Torres Gregory, *Journal of Philosophical Research*, vol. XXIII, 1998: 129–145.

Introduction

On the Way to Silence

This book charts the course of Heidegger's thoughts on silence, from *Being and Time* to *On the Way to Language*, and ends with critical conclusions mostly regarding his later conceptions (from the 1950s onward). In "A Dialogue on Language," Heidegger offers a clue to one of the main constants of his way to silence: "Above all, silence about silence . . . ."[1] The importance that he assigns to being silent (*Geschweigen*), keeping silent (*Schweigen*), hearkening (*Horchen*), and reticence (*Verschwiegenheit*), especially when silence itself is in question, is reflected in his meditations and sayings. In particular, he is often reticent when he speaks about silence, but he also tends to intimate what he deliberately leaves unsaid. So, my interpretation focuses on what he *says* as well as on what he does *not* say (and instead hints) concerning silence. In this dual focus, I make the effort to let him speak and intimate in his own words.

My working thesis is that silence, truth as the unhiddenness or unconcealedness (*Unverborgenheit*) of being (*Sein*)/beyng (*Seyn*), and language as sonorous saying (*Sage*) that shows (*Zeigen*) or as saying that discloses in word-sounds are continually interlinked in Heidegger. While he does not offer what would generally count as a "definition" of silence, it is never essentially a static, inert state characterized by the absence of sound, and sound itself is never essentially an acoustic object, tone datum, or abstract noise. Instead, silence is a sort of meaningful happening in and through which a multiplicity of occurrences unfold that pertain to sound and involve intricate plays of concealedness/unconcealedness and of showing in the manner of uncovering (*Entdeckung*) and covering up (*Verdeckung*). I claim that the links between silence, truth, and language hold, even as the concepts themselves morph in his path from the project of fundamental ontology and its Dasein-analytic to the thinking of being/beyng in the appropriating-event (*Er-eignis*).

I begin here by depicting Heidegger's concepts of silence, truth, and language in broad strokes to give a preliminary sense of my working thesis. I focus on truth understood as unconcealedness first because it remains fundamental in the conceptual interplay that develops over time. The basic meaning of truth as unconcealedness is that the being of beings or of what is (*Seiendes*) is originally concealed, so that *un*concealing involves a wresting away from an original concealedness. In this *un*concealing, beings become manifest; beings are what is unconcealed. Being itself emerges, revealing itself in its coming into presence or presencing (*Anwesung*). However, being, which is abyssally different from beings themselves, is at the same time concealed in the un*concealing*. In this sense, unconcealedness also involves the absencing (*Abwesung*) of being in which it withdraws into concealedness. The very process of unconceal*ing* or unconcealment as it unfolds conceals itself as well. The human being as Da-sein is the "there" (*Da*) where being unconceals itself through beings at the same time that it and its unconcealing conceal themselves. These are roughly the constants in the concept of truth in relation to silence and language as Heidegger's focus changes from Da-sein to being, to beyng as the difference between being and beings, and finally to the appropriating-event of the truth of beyng.

The idea of language as sonorous saying that shows or as saying that reveals in word-sounds serves to define the human being and to distinguish it from all other beings. Truth as unconcealedness is fundamental for the essentially human capacity to show in word-sounds what is unconcealed as well as what is concealed. Furthermore, language as sonorous speech can show in the manner of uncovering or of covering up what it shows. However, while Heidegger constantly assigns these sonorous showing capacities to speech, the meaning of the word "*Sprache*" (language) undergoes significant changes. At first, *Sprache* is the worldly expressedness (*Hinausgesprochenheit*) of Da-sein's discourse (*Rede*), which is the human being's essential capacity to show in the manner of meaningfully disclosing or letting something be seen as something. *Sprache* in this sense has its roots in *Rede*; language is discourse that is always already put into word-sounds; it is sonorous speech as a capacity and as the very activity of speaking. As Heidegger's focus changes, *Sprache* progressively takes on the meaning of the being, nature, or essence (*Wesen*) of language in relation to being/beyng and the appropriating-event. Understood as the essence of language, *Sprache* remains as a saying that shows, but it does not show in word-sounds, for it is soundless, that is, it is not sonorous. Instead, the sonorous showing, the saying that shows in word-sounds, becomes what defines the human essence. At times, the later Heidegger will make the distinction between language and its essence more evident by referring to the essence of language as the soundless saying, word, voice, or clearing (*Lichtung*) of being/beyng and the appropriating-event. In the later formulations, *Sprache* as soundless showing essentially involves truth, for language in its essence itself becomes the site of unconcealedness.

I claim that the idea of silence as a meaningful happening that pertains to sound and involves truth and language is always linked to unconcealedness and showing, but in many different and intricate ways. Silence in relation to sound is always something meaningful that happens, but *what* happens, *where* it happens, and *how* it happens changes in Heidegger's regard. At first, it is only the silence that belongs to Da-sein in its essential capacity to speak in word-sounds, that is, to its discourse and language. Silence in this sense pertains to the sonorous saying that shows, and it can take many forms with regard to speech and to speaking in word-sounds. As Heidegger's focus shifts to being/beyng and the appropriating-event, sound and silence acquire much deeper meanings, so that they themselves come to determine the human essence in terms of the sonorous saying that shows. The human being becomes the sonorous sayer. Sound takes on a more fundamental role as the sounding (*Lautung*) that enables the sonorous speech of the human being as the mortal who shows in word-sounds. Silence becomes more fundamentally a happening in the essence of language or in the word as the voice or the clearing of being/beyng and the appropriating-event. Silence in this sense pertains to the soundless showing of the word, through which language in its essence first lets beings be seen as beings. However, I maintain that there is an even deeper silence, which pertains to the stillness (*die Stille*), as the soundless origin of the word itself, that is, as the site from which the essence of language can arise. In Heidegger's later formulations, this deeper silence will belong to the appropriating-event of the truth of beyng, in which the word itself becomes the site of unconcealedness.

From the start, Heidegger's ideas of silence in its links with truth and language are quite intricate, taking on what I identify as three distinct forms, schematically as follows:

(A) Human silence: Applies to Da-sein and to the mortals of the fourfold (earth, sky, mortals, and immortals) in their sonorous saying that shows in word-sounds. It can occur when we refrain from speaking about certain things or from saying something in particular, when we withhold certain words or find ourselves at a loss for words, or when cannot say something for whatever reason. Authentic human silence includes being silent, keeping silent, hearkening, and reticence.

(B) Primordial silence: Applies to the essence of language as the soundless saying that shows or to the word as the silent voice or clearing of being/beyng. This silence is deeper than human silence in that it pertains to being/beyng and to language in its being.

(C) Primeval silence: Pertains to the stillness and to the originary concealedness of being/beyng; it is the deepest silence that determines all silences, including the primordial silence of the word and, ultimately, the human silence.

I also identify three different levels at which silence can occur in relation to language as sonorous speech, as follows:

(1) Linguistic: *In* language as sonorous saying that shows in word-sounds.
(2) Pre-linguistic: In what determines *language* as sonorous speech. This level includes (a) the earlier disclosedness (*Erschlossenheit*) of Dasein and (b) the later openness (*Offenheit*) of the mortals, as well as the essence of language as the soundless saying or the word as the voice or the clearing of being/beyng. While disclosedness and openness belong to the human being, the word belongs to being/beyng. So, this level may be marked by (A) human silence and (B) primordial silence.
(3) Proto-linguistic: In what determines the *essence* of language as the soundless saying that shows or the word as the clearing. At its deepest point, this is the level of the appropriating-event of the truth or unconcealedness of beyng, and it includes the stillness. Only (C) primeval silence marks this ultimate level.

The following figure shows how truth relates to the different forms of silence and levels in relation to language as sonorous speech:

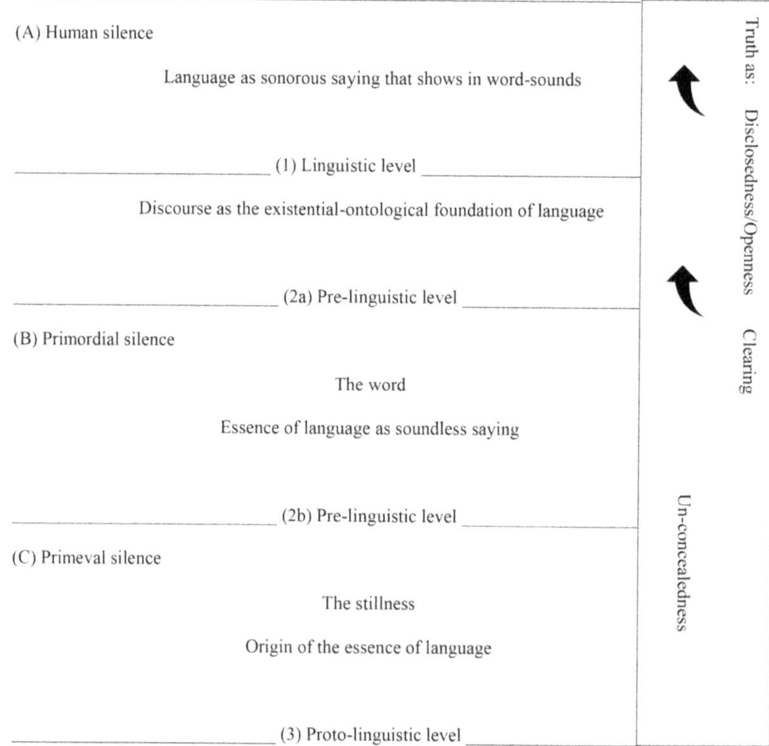

Figure 0.1

The different dynamics at play in Heidegger's concepts of silence infuse them with a remarkable vibrancy and complexity. The verbal sense of the word "*das Schweigen*" thus predominates in his vocabulary. Eventually, silencing (*Erschweigung*) and ultimately stilling (*stillen*) will prevail in the happening of silence as the stillness becomes for Heidegger the ultimate source from which sound breaks off and language originates.

The ongoing interplay between truth, language, and silence in Heidegger's reflections over time yields a profusion of ideas that form into quite unique concepts of silence. One of the features that make them distinctive is how they couple visual with aural tropes. The graphic dynamics of truth (from an original concealedness to an unconcealing that unconceals at the same time that it conceals) resonate in the relation between silence and sound. However, while there is certainly an association between hiddenness and silence on the one hand, and unhiddenness and sound on the other, there is not a simple one-to-one correlation. Thus, sound can operate as a concealing force and silence can have the power to unconceal as well.

The visual/aural couplings are also reflected in the sonorous showing or disclosure through word-sounds that constantly define human speech in Heidegger's reflections. However, since showing can take the forms of uncovering or of covering up, there is not a simple one-to-one correlation with regard to word-sounds and silence either. So, silence in speech can uncover something and word-sounds can cover something up. Heidegger's later focus on the question concerning the essence of language or the word as the clearing of beyng in its presencing and absencing, and as the saying of the event in its appropriating, adds to the complexity of the web of interrelations. In this sense, the word as the silent showing and as the soundless peal of the stillness unconceals and discloses at the same time that it conceals and covers up.

With the publication of Heidegger's *Schwarze Hefte (Black Notebooks)*, the issue of his public silence concerning the Holocaust in light of his anti-semitic and other chauvinist remarks has rekindled heated controversies over the intrinsic meaning and value of his thinking. However, the personal and political contextualization of Heidegger's thoughts on silence has tended to prevail over systematic inquiries into their inner workings. I focus on Heidegger's philosophical concept of silence as such to give a comprehensive view of its development, and I offer an in-depth analysis of its different formulations, without ignoring the problem of his affiliations with National Socialism. I also conclude with critical reflections on Heidegger's concept of silence in relation to a variety of themes, and I propose alternatives to the aspects that I identify as problematic, including its deafness to oppressive silencings.

In what follows, I offer a preview of the nine chapters that compose this book. The first eight chapters are the signposts marking Heidegger's way to silence, which reaches its greatest depths with the primordial and primeval forms. Chapter 9 points to paths that his way closes and paths that it may open up.

Chapter 1: "From the Silent Call of Conscience and Reticent Discourse to the Silencing in Dread and Profound Boredom in Da-sein": This chapter covers the period of 1927–29. I claim that in *Being and Time*, Da-sein's disclosedness, which is for Heidegger the primordial phenomenon of truth as unconcealedness, is the pre-linguistic basis for his existential-ontological concept of silence. Heidegger focuses on human silence and construes it only as a possibility of discourse, which he places at both the linguistic and the pre-linguistic levels with his definition of language as its worldly expressedness. I identify two forms of authentic discourse—the primary form of Da-sein in relation to its self and a secondary form of authentic dialogue. I also claim that, while Heidegger gives special attention to silence in relation to the call of conscience and the reticence of authentic discourse, silence operates in the inauthentic idle talk (*Gerede*) as well. Moreover, silence can involve covering up in both authentic and inauthentic discourse.

Turning to "What Is Metaphysics?" and *The Fundamental Concepts of Metaphysics: World, Finitude, Solitude,* I maintain that Heidegger begins to interpret silence in a closer relation to the truth of being in his discussions of the fundamental attunements or moods (*Grundstimmungen*) of dread or anxiety (*Angst*) and of boredom (*Langeweiligkeit*). I also claim that while there are important differences between these works and *Being and Time*, for example, in what is revealed in the fundamental attunements, silence and language are still grounded in Da-sein's being.

Chapter 2: "Toward the Essence of Silence": In the early 1930s, we witness significant changes in Heidegger's concepts of truth and language as he begins to inquire into their respective essences, their relation to beings as a whole, and their relation to the being of beings. His concept of silence also shifts when he identifies keeping silent as the origin of discourse and language. This chapter focuses mainly on two courses where the evolving links between these concepts are most evident.

The first course I consider is "On the Essence of Truth" in 1933–34, where Heidegger explicitly defines the ability to keep silent as the origin and the ground of language. I maintain that this definition remains focused on the pre-linguistic level of Da-sein's truth, even as he centers on the truth of being and the revelation of beings as a whole in language, insofar as he concentrates on human silence.

It is in the second course, the 1934 summer course *Logic as the Question Concerning the Essence of Language*, that Heidegger takes a more decisive step toward the essence of silence in relation to being through his idea of language as the world-forming power (*weltbildende Macht*). While he remains entrenched, for the most part, in Da-sein's keeping silent as he develops the idea of language in relation to lore (*Kunde*), Heidegger also hints at a deeper silence by connecting lore to the mystery (*Geheimnis*) of being. Both courses are heavily charged with fascist ideological terms and references to the political context at the time, so I also explore their bearing on his concept of silence.

Chapter 3: "The Poetics of Silence in a Dialogue with Hölderlin": This chapter focuses on Heidegger's 1934–35 interpretation of Hölderlin in *Hölderlin's Hymns "Germania" and "The Rhein."* I claim that Heidegger's own poetics of silence finds its reticent expression in his reading of the poems. More specifically, my contention is that he sees silence here at the pre-linguistic level as the origin of language and he begins to see language itself in an intimate relation with truth as the site of the originary unveiling of beyng. I show how he develops his distinction between idle talk and the keeping silent and reticent telling of the poets and thinkers by using Hölderlin's poetic images of the human being as a dialogue and of language as the most dangerous of goods. The silences of gods and demigods in Hölderlin's poems add more nuances to Heidegger's concept of human silence. However, it is in his reading of "The Rhein" that he brings forth his idea of the primeval silence of beyng as the origin of language in its essence. He formulates this origin in terms of the mystery of beyng, which pertains to concealedness. I discuss how the silencing power of the mystery is linked with the concealedness into which beyng withdraws in its refusal (*Versagung*). I also examine how the poetic co-respondence (*Ent-sprechung*) with this mystery takes form as a profound reticence and is based on an authentic form of hearing that Heidegger identifies as originary.

Chapter 4: "Sigetics and the Silence of the Other Beginning in the Appropriating-Event": This chapter focuses mostly on the 1936–38 manuscript *Contributions to Philosophy (Of the Event),* where Heidegger initiates the project of the transition from metaphysics to the thinking of the truth of beyng in the event of appropriation. I discuss the different forms of silence that unfold in the event and in the thinking that is appropriated in the event in light of his definition of truth in terms of clearing-concealing (*Lichtung und Verbergung*). The thoughtful speaking of *sigetics* (from the ancient Greek "*sigaō*," meaning "to keep or to be silent") bears silence and is reticent in its co-respondence with the primordial silence of the word and the primeval silence of beyng. The fundamental attitudes of restraint, shock, and diffidence, and the fundamental disposition of stillness, which involves the ability to hear and to be silent, are all interlinked. I claim that the thinking in the crossing faces two abyssal silences as it makes the attempt to say the language of beings as the language of beyng. Heidegger tries to adhere to his own sigetic principles, so my interpretation focuses as well on what he intimates about the deeper silences of beyng and the word when he identifies silence as the ground and origin of language in its essence.

Chapter 5: "The Silent Origin of Language in the Confrontation with Herder": In this chapter, I show how Heidegger's 1939 seminar *On the Essence of Language. The Metaphysics of Language and the Essencing of the Word. Concerning Herder's Treatise* On the Origin of Language serves as another passageway on his way to silence. The word as the origin (*Ursprung*) of language, as the ground of its essence (*Wesensgrund*), and as the essencing (*Wesung*) of the truth of beyng marks the confrontation with Herder's metaphysical origination (*Enstehung*) of language in the reflective awareness (*Besonnenheit*) of the rational animal. At the same time, I show how Herder's (unwitting) sense of the ear as "the first teacher of language" serves as a springboard for Heidegger's development of the deeper sense of the hearkening that defines the human essence in its silencing (*Erschweigen*) in relation to the primordial silence of the word. Heidegger also launches his deeper sense of "sounding" in terms of the word as the clearing through his critique of Herder's notion of language as the "sounding of reason." I claim that Heidegger hints at the primeval silence of beyng in his comments on the rending (*Zerreibung*) of silence and the refusal of beyng as it withdraws into concealedness. I also show how these hints become more explicit as he interprets the last verse of Stephan George's poem "The Word": "No thing may be where the word does break."

Chapter 6: "Toward the Originary Logic of Silence in a Translation of Heraclitus": The main focus of this chapter is Heidegger's 1944 summer seminar "Logic: Heraclitus's Doctrine of the *Logos*," where his stated aim is to arrive at an originary logic—a thinking that reflects on and belongs to the *Logos*—through the translation of Heraclitus. I maintain that Heidegger advances his reflections on silence or quiescence in relation to the appropriating-event of the truth of beyng through his silent trans-lation (*Übersetzung*) of what Heraclitus reticently said, did not say, and could not say about the *Logos*. Claiming that the Greeks did not think the essence of *alētheia* as the unconcealedness of being, Heidegger establishes the links of the *Logos* (thought in its originary form) to the truth of beyng. In my analysis of the complex interplay that Heidegger develops regarding quiescence, I identify the three major players: The *Logos* as being in its forgathering (*Versammlung*); the human *logos* in its gathering (*Sammlung*); and *Alētheia* as unconcealedness—or, ultimately, the truth of beyng in the event. I also identify eight different forms of quiescence, which focus first on the human being's relation to *Logos* and end with the stillness in which the truth of beyng shelters itself. I show how these forms correlate with the deeper (primordial and primeval) forms of silence and their corresponding pre-linguistic and proto-linguistic levels.

Chapter 7: "Quiet Musings in the Project toward the Stillness": This chapter focuses on Heidegger's *Zum Wesen der Sprache und Zur Frage nach der Kunst* (*On the Essence of Language and On the Question Concerning Art*), which includes previously unpublished writings dating from the 1940s to 1960. Heidegger's quiet musings on the essence of language probe deeper into the primeval silence of beyng that pertains to the stillness. My interpretation of his project toward the stillness first centers on his fragmentary and elliptical sayings in prose. I identify the three forms of silence (human, primordial, and primeval) and the multiple dimensions in which they operate with regard to saying and the truth of beyng in the appropriating-event. I also develop how Heidegger's characterization of the stillness as the first word or the fore-word (*Vor-wort*) of beyng and as the abyssal-ground (*Ab-grund*) of the appropriating-event allows us to see more into its relations to the truth and the word of beyng. These characterizations are reflected in his poem "Die Geburt der Sprache" (The Birth of Language), which I claim is sigetic and conceals the stillness in its attempt to co-respond with the primeval silence.

Chapter 8: "The Soundless Peal of the Stillness": This chapter ends my account of Heidegger's way to silence with the collection of essays from the 1950s that compose his *Unterwegs zur Sprache* (five of which are translated in *On the Way to Language* and one in *Poetry, Language, Thought*). Heidegger makes no explicit references to the truth of beyng, choosing instead to focus on the appropriation of the mortals for the sonorous saying, and on different configurations of disclosure that unfold with the essence of language. I claim that the idea of language as the soundless peal (*Geläut*) of the stillness in particular captures well the dynamic of truth as its plays out in the interrelation between the primeval silence that belongs to the stillness, the primordial silence of the peal, and the human silence in hearkening and reticent co-respondence. I show in detail how the dynamic of the clearing-concealing of beyng is at play, and I trace its relation to the three forms of silence (human, primordial, and primeval) in Heidegger's different formulations of the disclosive essence of language.

Chapter 9: "Sounding Out the Later Meanings of Silence": In this final chapter, I undertake a critical reflection on the later Heidegger's concept of silence in three sections. In the first section, I contend that he effectively renders silence relative to the sonorous speech that he claims has its origin in the primeval and primordial silences. This relation is not circular, but it either reduces all forms of attunement to silence to linguistic forms or excludes the possibility of non-linguistic attunements, as in instrumental music. I also question that it manages to overcome the metaphysical sensible/supersensible distinction and to capture our embodied existence.

In the second section, I critically examine Heidegger's view of poetry and thinking as the only authentic forms of experiencing profound silence. My position is that while he rejects mysticism as metaphysical, a deeper sense of "mysticism" is possible as a non-metaphysical form of experiencing the silent mystery of beyng, and it can be found exemplified in his own writing practices. I also claim that, though he constantly associates everyday discourse with loud idle talk, there are rare instances in which he acknowledges the possibility of authentic dialogues and silences in the everyday. In this light, I question the coherence of his hierarchization and distinction between authentic and inauthentic experiences.

In the third and final section, I focus on Heidegger's portrayal of the mortals of the fourfold as the only beings who are needed for their sonorous saying. The divine realm is thus centered on the human in this anthropocentric depiction. The role of the immortals in their silent calls and answers is defined entirely in terms of the linguistic essence of the mortals. The only sonorous voice in the fourfold is that of the mortals, because animals as well as gods are incapable of sonorous speech. In this regard, I question his view of animal sonorousness as devoid of meaning. In closing, I turn to his depiction of the silencing of the earth and the deforming of human essence into the technologized animal in the loud age of machination (*Machenschaft*) and en-framing or framing (*Ge-stell*). I maintain that there are more positive possibilities of profound silence in the technological everyday than he envisioned. His call for releasement (*Gelassenheit*) with regard to technological things is one example of how some of those possibilities can be realized.

NOTES

1. Martin Heidegger, "A Dialogue on Language," in *On the Way to Language*, trans. Peter D. Hertz (New York: Harper & Row, 1971), 52 / US, 152.

Chapter 1

From the Silent Call of Conscience and Reticent Discourse to the Silencing in Dread and Profound Boredom in Da-sein

This chapter, which is divided in two sections, initiates my working thesis concerning the links between Heidegger's concepts of silence, truth as unhiddenness, and language as sonorous showing. In section 1.1, I propose to explore *Being and Time*, where Heidegger focuses on Da-sein's disclosedness as the primordial phenomenon of truth. I aim to prove that disclosedness, which takes the form of uncovering, serves as the pre-linguistic basis for the existential-ontological concept of silence that he develops in terms of the voice of conscience and reticent discourse. My main objective in section 1.2 is to prove that Heidegger begins to conceptualize silence in the more direct relation to the unconcealedness of being in its presencing/absencing as he develops his 1929 analyses of the fundamental attunements of dread—in "What is Metaphysics?"—and profound boredom—in *The Fundamental Concepts of Metaphysics: World, Finitude, Solitude*. The chapter concludes in this section with a comparison between the concepts of silence in these works and *Being and Time*, which I maintain still concern the human form of silence.

1.1. THE SILENT CALL OF CONSCIENCE AND RETICENT DISCOURSE

Heidegger's definition of truth as unconcealedness is fundamental to the concept of silence that he develops solely with explicit reference to Da-sein in *Being and Time*. Truth in its original sense "must always *first* be wrested from" beings, which get "snatched out of their hiddenness."[1] The original concealedness of the being of beings as what "remains *hidden* in the most egregious sense," the unconcealment of beings, and the derivative concealedness of being in which it gets "covered up again" or "shows itself only 'in disguise,'" determine the very possibility of Da-sein's disclosedness.[2] It is within truth as unconcealedness that disclosedness as the uncovering and covering up of what is unconcealed and of what is concealed is itself possible. However, at this stage in Heidegger, silence does not explicitly pertain to the truth of being, but to disclosedness as the phenomenon of truth, that is, to Da-sein as the "there" of being, as the site of the showing of beings in which being hides itself. More specifically, silence is a possibility only of discourse, though Da-sein's hearing, keeping silent, and reticence all draw their force from the unconcealing and concealing power of the truth of the being of beings.[3] In fact, as I will later prove, silence can take more forms than those that Heidegger explicitly associates with authenticity, and they can involve covering up as well as the obvious uncovering that unfolds in resoluteness.

Da-sein's disclosive possibilities are enacted in the equiprimordial existentialia that constitute its being-in-the-world (state-of-mind or mood, understanding and its development in interpretation, and discourse). The existentialia thus operate equiprimordially in the disclosedness that takes form in Da-sein's being-true as being-uncovering (truth in the first sense) and the being-true of beings within the world as being-uncovered (truth in the second sense).[4] At the same time, insofar as disclosedness also involves covering up, I claim that there would be two corresponding senses of being-untrue though Heidegger does not explicitly mention them.

The first sense of being-untrue would be Da-sein's covering up, while the second would be the being-covered up of beings within the world. The second sense could apply to any case in which beings are uncovered as what they are not, as in discourse that says something false, for example. Heidegger considers this general case when he argues that for the ancient Greeks, the *logos*, which he translates as "*Rede*" (discourse), is true when it lets something be seen "as something unhidden (*alēthes*)" and it is false when it covers up something, "passing it off *as* something which it is *not*."[5] The first sense of being-untrue corresponds to what Heidegger designates as Da-sein's "untruth" in its falling, which consists in its "being closed off and covered up," its "*facticity*."[6] Furthermore, both ways of being-untrue are grounded in Da-sein's disclosedness. The two senses of covering up (applied to Da-sein and to the beings within its world) are thus grounded in Da-sein's original uncovering. As I now hope to show, they operate in the different forms that silence can take in Da-sein.

Focusing on discourse, we see that the role that it plays in disclosedness is to articulate the intelligibility of being-in-the-world in terms of the totality of words (language) that accrue to the meanings or significations, which themselves form a whole (the-totality-of-significations). Discourse performs this disclosive role, specifically by verbalizing or putting into words Da-sein's mood and understanding about something as something. Heidegger takes pains to explain that the communication or explicit sharing that takes place in discourse is grounded in the being-with-one-another, the shared conversance of being-in-the world, which develops into talking and listening to one another.[7] He also emphasizes that vocal utterance, that is, sonorous expression or communication in word-sounds, is not a necessary characteristic of discourse. In the original sense of *logos* as discourse that makes manifest (*dēloun*) and lets something be seen from itself (*apophansis*), it is only when "fully concrete" that discoursing or talking "has the character of speaking [*Sprechens*]—vocal proclamation in words" or of "*phonē meta phantasias*—an utterance in which something is sighted in each case."[8] Conversely, then, discourse has the possibility of silence in the sense of *a-phonē*, that is, of soundless or non-sonorous disclosure when it is *not* fully concrete or vocalized. Put otherwise, discourse can be silent by not speaking or uttering word-sounds about something.

Language in its existential-ontological sense is the worldly expressedness of discourse and as such "already *hides* in itself a developed way of conceiving."[9] It follows that the "hidden" understanding and interpretation remain silent, even as discourse uncovers what is understood and what is interpreted in its worldly form as language. Insofar as Heidegger attributes to language the intrinsic function of hiding, this silence as a covering up of understanding and interpretation always already goes with verbalized and/or vocalized discourse, that is, in the words and/or word-sounds of its worldly expressedness as language.

It is worth noting that the forms of discursive silence that I have pointed out so far apply to discourse in general, that is, independently of its (authentic or inauthentic) mode. Generally speaking, Heidegger explains that disclosedness "pertains equiprimordially to the world, to Being-in, and to the Self."[10] As a possibility that belongs to discourse, then, silence can occur in such disclosures. More generally, regardless of the mode of discourse and its particular type of disclosure, silence can concern beings, beings as a whole, being in general, and Da-sein's own self in its being-in-the-world.

Turning first to the inauthentic mode of discourse—idle talk, we find that everyday Da-sein covers up both the beings that it uncovers within its world as well as its own self. Generally speaking, in the falling into the world, what "has been uncovered and disclosed stands in a mode in which it has been disguised and closed off by idle talk, curiosity, and ambiguity."[11] Given its focus on what is said in a talk, idle talk directs Da-sein away from a "primordial" understanding toward an "average" understanding of what the talk is about. In this manner, idle talking and listening to idle talk leads, through gossiping and passing the word along, to the groundlessness and the average intelligibility in which nothing seems to be closed off. Idle talk thus appears here to offer endless possibilities for uncovering beings, but instead "amounts to perverting the act of disclosing [*Erschliessen*] into an act of closing off [*Verschliessen*]."[12] I claim that it is through this act of closing off that idle talk in effect imposes silence with regard to the beings talked about by treating them as something that we already understand and have no need to inquire into any further.

A similar form of silencing occurs with regard to the self in the everyday being-in-the world, which Heidegger describes as "the real dictatorship of the 'they.'"[13] Da-sein's disclosive possibilities in relation to its own being pertain to its being as a self. In its everyday being-with, it is the inauthentic they-self, which Heidegger markedly distinguishes from the authentic being-one's-self. The authentic self has taken hold of and is its own self. In contrast, Da-sein's everyday way of being-in-the-world involves missing and covering itself up. Specifically in the idle talk of the they, Da-sein is severed from all of its authentic relationships, including how it relates to its own self. Da-sein thereby floats unattached to anything, but this occurs always by floating toward itself. However, with the averageness of the interpretations by the they, "the uncanniness of this floating remains hidden from it under their protecting shelter."[14] In hiding the uncanniness, the they occludes the authentic mood in which Da-sein is "anxious with anxiety about its ownmost potentiality-for-being." I claim that, in this manner, idle talk here silences in that it covers up by *drowning out* the call that "discourses in the uncanny mode of keeping silent."[15]

The soundless call of conscience can be covered up in idle talk in different ways. One way of covering up occurs with the "loud" chatter of the they, which drowns out the authentic keeping silent and reticence. Another form of silencing consists in the fact that the they not only talks loudly but also incessantly, in its constant pursuit of things that spark its curiosity. Furthermore, idle talk silences by withholding talk about authentic existential experiences in mood and understanding concerning anxiety, being-towards-death, keeping silent, reticence, and resoluteness. The use of the phrases "one dies" and "it was really nothing" when anxiety subsides exemplify these forms of inauthentic silencing.[16] Inauthentic discourse can cover up Da-sein's potentiality-for-being itself by presenting Da-sein's possibilities in vague and ambiguous ways.[17] The they's received view of conscience in its silent call is a form of inauthentic silencing insofar as the call is interpreted as something that is not present-at-hand and the they thereby "covers up its own failure to hear the call."[18] Correspondingly, the inauthentic hearing, which is a "hearing something 'all around' [*Das Nur-herum-hören*] is a privation" of the authentic hearing, covering up the possibility of hearkening to the silent call of conscience.[19] Thus, "[l]osing itself in the publicness and the idle talk of the 'they,'" Da-sein "fails to hear [*überhört*] its own Self in listening to the they-self."[20]

The hiding, covering up, and closing off that characterize the inauthentic silence of idle talk is what I identify as a form of *muzzling* and *staying mum* about the authentic possibilities of being-in-the-world. These are possibilities only insofar as Da-sein is equiprimordially in the truth and in the untruth.[21] If the phenomenon of truth in its most primordial sense is Da-sein's disclosedness, then inauthentic silence is still a form of disclosure, albeit one that, like idle talk, would amount to a closing off. However, such perversion and distortion are only possible because Da-sein is equiprimordially in the untruth, that is, in the covering up that goes with uncovering in the inauthentic everydayness of falling. In this sense, the inauthentic silence that goes with idle talk uncovers solely in the mode of covering up.

That Heidegger considers the possibility of an inauthentic silence is also evident when he uses (existentiell) examples of talkative, mute, and taciturn persons to highlight the special character of authentic keeping silent in everyday conversations. The talkative type covers up what they chatter about bringing it to "a sham clarity—the unintelligibility of the trivial," while the person who keeps silent can bring us to a more authentic understanding. However, neither the mute person nor the taciturn type is able to prove that they can keep silent in the authentic sense. In this regard, Heidegger highlights here how authentic keeping silent is based on having "something to say," which involves an "authentic and rich" self-disclosedness and thereby can contribute to an authentic uncovering with others.[22]

The form of authentic keeping silent and reticence that occurs in dialogues with others and involves a break from the covering up of idle talk is secondary. It presupposes the primary form of authentic keeping silent in the hearkening to the silent call of conscience and the reticent resoluteness of the Da-sein that becomes its own self. Put otherwise, only the person who has uncovered and reticently resolved their authentic being one's self in the existential soliloquy of their conscience can also uncover things in reticent conversations with others. It is worth noting that the possibility of an authentic reticent talk with others about other things besides oneself in the with-world of falling is a rare exception in Heidegger's general rule of focusing here on everyday discourse in terms of the inauthentic idle talk.

Turning now to the primary form of authentic keeping silent and reticence, we find that it is characterized by the silencing, not only of the idle talk of the inauthentic they but also of language altogether as the worldly expressedness and vocalization of discourse in word-sounds. The silencing of idle talk occurs in the call of conscience, which "does not call [Da-sein] into the public idle talk of the 'they.'"[23] Moreover, in the call itself, idle talk is silenced insofar as the "constant Being-guilty is represented, and in this way the Self is brought back from the loud idle talk which goes with the common sense of the 'they.'"[24] The silencing of what is linguistic or verbal is another feature of the call, insofar as it "does not put itself into words at all," and "what is called in the call has not been formulated in words."[25]

However, Heidegger himself still formulates the call of conscience as a pronouncement in the sentence "Guilty!" as he conveys the idea that being-guilty belongs to Da-sein's being.[26] This apparent inconsistency can easily be resolved by realizing that the sentence plays a role in the phenomenological description of the experience. In my view, what is more problematic is his conflation of language with idle talk, for this is what most likely leads him to deny verbalization and vocalization to the call. In fact, he connects the call's silencing of what is verbal with the silencing of idle talk by "tak[ing] the words away from" it. The call silences all that is sonorous in language as well, for it not only "dispenses with any kind of utterance [*Verlautbarung*]" or vocalization, but the discourse of conscience in general also "never comes to utterance." Heidegger also characterizes here the uncanny discursive mode of keeping silent in the call of conscience as non-sonorous when he claims that "the call comes from the soundlessness of uncanniness."[27]

In contrast with the ambiguity and sham clarity that occur in the covering up in inauthentic discourse, the silent call of conscience remains "nothing less than obscure and indefinite" in its uncovering.[28] Heidegger takes pains to highlight the clarity and distinctness of the call: The call does not have "the indefiniteness of a mysterious voice" and it is not as if Da-sein were "assailed by some 'obscure power.'"[29] Though caller and called are both indefinite, the caller reaches the called one with "a cold assurance, which is uncanny but by no means obvious." Moreover, here this uncanny assurance has its basis in the fact that Da-sein "has been individualized down to itself in its uncanniness," so that there is no room for itself "to be mistaken for anything else."[30] It is in the silent "appeal" that Da-sein "gives itself to understand its ownmost potentiality-for-Being."[31] So, the call of conscience in its silence is like a light that inexorably exposes the self to itself in the nudity of its unrealized potentiality-for-being one's self.

The inexorability of the self-exposure in the silent call of conscience is reflected in the fact that the call "forces the Dasein which has been appealed to and summoned, into the reticence of itself" and "*calls* him *back* from" the they in its idle talk "*into the reticence of his existent* potentiality-for-Being."[32] The silent call of conscience is thus a force that compels Da-sein into reticence, which Heidegger defines as the authentic form of discourse in "wanting to have a conscience."[33] Unlike the secondary form of reticence that can occur in an authentic talking with one another, this primary form of reticence involves no talking at all with others and evidently no "communication" whatsoever.[34]

The radical individualization in the silence that exposes Da-sein to itself and attunes it in the fundamental mood of anxiety in effect isolates it, "discloses it as '*solus ipse*.'"[35] In the primary form of reticence, Da-sein silences itself, not only in the sense of closing off the possibility of a "counter-discourse" but also in the deeper sense of opening itself to its own truth by hearkening to the call, whereby "hearing has appropriated the content of the call unconcealedly."[36]

The deepest silence lies within Da-sein, in what Heidegger refers to as "the stillness of itself" and identifies as that to which it is "called back" and "called back as something that is to become still." Here, the stillness is not merely the quietude and serenity of the self that withdraws into itself, away from the bustle and loudness of the they in its idle talk. It is fundamentally the silence of Da-sein in the nullity of its being. The self that it is *not* lies hidden within—it is the ownmost potentiality of being one's self.[37] In this sense, the call to the stillness of itself is a call *away* from the inauthentic self. It calls *back* and *toward* the authentic self. For all its disclosiveness and transparency with regard to Da-sein's self-being, reticence involves not only a withdrawal into a concealment from the they but also a sort of covering up that differs from the inauthentic covering up that distorts. The authentic covering up that occurs in reticence is instead a sheltering that preserves the self in its ownmost potentiality-for-being, protecting it *from* the they-self. In contrast, in being the they-self, Da-sein "for the most part remains concealed from itself in its authenticity."[38]

In the struggle of wresting itself away from the inauthentic they-self, Da-sein continues to be reticent in its disclosedness as it projects itself upon its ownmost being-guilty and makes itself ready for anxiety. This moment of reticent self-projection in readiness for anxiety is what Heidegger defines as "resoluteness."[39] In *Erschlossenheit* (disclosedness), then, *Entschlossenheit* (resoluteness) is the unlocking and unveiling of the self that lies hidden in the stillness of itself. Reticent resoluteness is thus the keeping silent about Da-sein's deepest silence—its primordial self, which it has taken hold of and made its own in being-guilty.[40]

The reticence that involves concealing and covering up one's self from the they-self characterizes resoluteness as well. Reticent resoluteness is thereby an unveiling of the self to itself that, at the same time, veils the self from the they-self. This reticent withholding of one's self takes discursive form as a wordless self-affirmation: "As something that keeps silent, authentic being-one's-Self is just the sort of thing that does not keep on saying 'I'; but in its reticence it 'is' that thrown entity as which it can authentically [*be*]."[41] Reticence is a mark of the authentic resoluteness that takes form in what Heidegger defines as anticipatory resoluteness, where Da-sein in its understanding of its ownmost potentiality of being "will go right under the eyes of Death" in taking over its thrownness.[42] In this sense, the authentic being-towards-death in which Da-sein unveils itself to itself in its finitude continues to veil itself from the they. The double movement of unveiling and veiling applies to fate (*Schicksal*), which Heidegger defines as "that powerless superior power" in which Da-sein "reticently" stands ready for anxiety. Ultimately, then, the silent veiling-unveiling in reticence applies in authentic Da-sein's being as care and its ontological meaning as temporality and historicality, specifically with regard to its own "death, guilt, conscience, freedom, and finitude."[43]

In conclusion, *Being and Time* presents multiple possibilities of human silence in Da-sein that apply to both authentic and inauthentic discourse, and they involve various forms of uncovering and covering up in Da-sein's truth and untruth, as follows:

(A) Inauthentic possibilities of silence—covering up of what is uncovered.
  (1) Language hides understanding and interpretation.
  (2) Idle talk closes off possibilities of uncovering:
    a) Imposes silence about beings talked about;
    b) Drowns out the call of conscience through loud and incessant chatter and hearing all-around;
    c) Muzzles and stays mum about Da-sein's authentic experiences and possibilities (dictatorship of the they).
(B) Authentic possibilities of silence—uncovering *and* protective covering up of Da-sein's own self.
  (1) The call of conscience:
    a) Silencing of idle talk;
    b) Silencing of language;
    c) Silencing of counter-discourse;
    d) Keeping silent and hearkening.
  (2) Secondary form of reticence (in authentic dialogue with others).
  (3) Primary form of reticence (in existential soliloquy and anticipatory resoluteness).
  (4) Stillness of the self.

The distinctively human form of silence here is linked with language as the expressedness of discourse, which operates as showing in its function of making manifest, and with truth as the unhiddenness of which Da-sein's disclosedness is a phenomenon. Silence in these terms has its ultimate determination at the pre-linguistic level of disclosedness.

1.2. THE SILENCING IN DREAD AND PROFOUND BOREDOM

Heidegger's interpretation of silence in relation to Da-sein's being undergoes some subtle, though significant changes after *Being and Time* as he begins to make explicit the role that being itself in its unconcealedness plays in Da-sein's disclosedness. The silences that are possible in Da-sein's truth and untruth thus start to show in bolder lines the imprint of the truth of being. His discussion of dread or anxiety in his 1927 inaugural lecture "What is Metaphysics?" differs in some important respects from his analysis of Da-sein's fundamental mood of anxiety and his depiction of the reticent anticipatory resoluteness in which it stands ready for anxiety. I will focus on these changes in his approach to the attunement of dread to show how they have a bearing in his interpretation of silence. I will then show how his analysis of boredom in the 1929 course *The Fundamental Concepts of Metaphysics: World, Finitude, Solitude* continues to reflect his evolving thoughts on fundamental attunements and silence.

Aside from the obvious differences between one overarching goal and another—the Dasein-analytic in the project of fundamental ontology and the questioning of metaphysics in relation to the nothing, we can see that what dread itself discloses differs from one context to another. In *Being and Time*, dread reveals Da-sein "as Being-possible," in its "Being towards its ownmost potentiality-for-Being."[44] In "What is Metaphysics?," dread or anxiety reveals the nothing that itself nihilates, in which nihilation "the original openness of beings as such arises: that they are beings—and not nothing."[45] Heidegger portrays the nothing that is revealed in anxiety "as belonging to the being of beings" and as "originally belong[ing]" to the "essential unfolding" of beings "as such."[46] In *Being and Time*, in contrast, Da-sein's nullity is at the heart of the being-possible that dread reveals, but it is the existential-ontological nothingness of being-in-the-world, which is that in the face of which and that about which Da-sein experiences dread. The "It is nothing and nowhere" that is revealed in this experience, remains in the "obstinacy of the 'nothing and nowhere within-the-world,'" that is, "the world as such" of being-in-the-world.[47]

I claim that in the shift from the nullity of Da-sein to the nothing of being, Heidegger still retains the focus on Da-sein's silence, but he ascribes the silencing *power*, not to a call of conscience, but to the nihilating of the nothing itself: "Because beings as a whole slip away so that precisely the nothing crowds around, all utterance of the 'is' falls silent in the face of the nothing."[48] In this particular kind of silencing, it is the nothing that in its "wholly repelling gesture toward beings that are slipping away as a whole . . . pushes in on Dasein in anxiety."[49] In what Heidegger characterizes as the silencing of all "is," we are still able to express how we feel, and we can ask, though not answer, "What is 'it' that makes 'one' feel uncanny?"[50] The silence in which anxiety reveals the "no hold on things" thus pertains to our inability to utter an "is," to say the "it" as the being of all that is. This is because being itself remains hidden, even as "the nihilation of the nothing in general, and therewith the nothing itself, is disengaged from concealment." The unconcealedness of being in beings here unfolds in the nihilating of the nothing, insofar as "[for] human Dasein, the nothing makes possible the manifestness of beings as such." So, though Heidegger continues to interpret silence in human terms, here it is the "original manifestness of the nothing" in anxiety that defines the possibility of this silence.[51]

In his portrayal of the human openness in which "the originary anxiety in Dasein is usually repressed," Heidegger depicts two possible responses that are reminiscent of inauthentic idle talk and authentic reticent resoluteness.[52] In the first type of reaction, there is an attempt to cover up what dread reveals: "That in the uncanniness of anxiety, we often try to shatter the vacant stillness with compulsive talk only proves the presence of the nothing."[53] This empty stillness that is experienced in anxiety is the nihilating of the nothing itself. Though Heidegger does not explicitly connect this stillness to silence, it harks back to Da-sein's stillness of itself and dimly anticipates the later stilling of the stillness that belongs to the primeval silence of beyng. At this point, he portrays how chatter attempts to stifle anxiety, in its "breath," which "quivers perpetually through Da-sein, only slightly in what makes us jittery, imperceptibly in the 'Oh, yes' and the 'Oh, no' of men of affairs."[54] He also highlights how the nothing is leveled down in the averageness in which "we rattle off" the word "nothing" in our everyday chatter, treating it as "obvious" in its so-called definition as "the complete negation of the totality of beings."[55] This everyday talk allegedly reflects the inadequate attitudes of science, which in its ambivalence wants to know nothing of the nothing, and of the logic that dominates in metaphysics and defines the nothing in terms of the negation.[56]

In Heidegger's depiction of the authentic attitude, reticence and anticipatory resoluteness reappear under a new guise. Anxiety is "most readily in the reserved, and most assuredly in those who are basically daring," which are those who are "sustained by that on which they expend themselves—in order thus to preserve the ultimate grandeur of Dasein."[57] I claim that the reserve of those who open themselves up to the nihilating of the nothing in dread marks the human correspondence to a silencing that is deeper than that of the call of care, beyond the radical individualization of Da-sein and its taking hold of its ownmost potentiality-for-being. Reservedness is now instead the correspondence to the nihilating of the nothing. Similarly, the risk of those who offer themselves up to the nihilating of the nothing runs far ahead and beyond the authentic being-toward-death in which Da-sein unveils itself in its finitude. The risk is now instead involved in the metaphysical question that puts all into the question concerning the finitude of being itself: Why is there something rather than nothing? This risk hides and thereby preserves itself in a deeper keeping silent than that of Da-sein's reticence in its response to the call of care. In the deeper reticence, anxiety is "in secret alliance with the cheerfulness and gentleness of creative longing."[58] Thus, there are multiple layers of silence that harbor these authentic moods in their secret alliance and conceal them from the everyday and its chatter. Their common yearning for creativity suggests not only that these moods are anticipatory but also resolute in their projection toward new and original disclosures. In addition, Heidegger's mention of "authentic" or "profound" boredom and of joy as moods of disclosure in which we find ourselves among beings as a whole, suggests that they can themselves be harbored in silence. His comparison of profound boredom to a "muffling fog" suggests further that these authentic moods involve an overpowering silencing.[59] As I will now prove, these properties are confirmed, at least for what Heidegger some years later also calls "profound boredom."

In the *Fundamental Concepts of Metaphysics*, Heidegger distinguishes between three forms of boredom in terms of how they relate to the passing of time and their structural moments, which consist in being held in limbo and being left empty. The first two forms of boredom—becoming bored by and being bored with—are inauthentic moods in which idle talk prevails. The third form—"It is boring for one" is the only authentic mood—profound boredom—and it is accordingly characterized by an overpowering silencing as well as by a corresponding keeping silent and reticence.

Focusing first on the inauthentic forms of boredom, we find that becoming bored by is characterized by our being left empty by a particular thing that we find boring (a station where we are waiting for our train to arrive) and we are held in limbo by time, which drags on, as we seek to pass the time by driving it on. Heidegger claims that the inauthentic "*everyday* speaking, comportment and judgment" give expression to this superficial form of boredom in which we say "that things themselves, people themselves, events and places themselves are *boring*."[60] The second form of boredom, being bored with is an indefinite boredom pertaining to a situation (as when we have spent an evening at a party). In the everyday talk, we refer to this indeterminacy of our boredom as an "I know not what." In being bored with, the being left empty comes from us, as we abandon ourselves to what passes in time. We are held in limbo by time in its standing as we feel ourselves stuck in the now. In Heidegger's example, inauthentic idle talk plays a more significant role: We "chatter" as we let ourselves go, so that this "chattering away is a making present of whatever is taking place" and in our being "[w]holly present, we bring time to a stand."[61] I maintain that idle talk can play an equally decisive role in becoming bored by, as when we strike up a conversation about the train schedule with a stranger at the station just to pass the time by driving it on.

In the profound boredom in which "It is boring for one," passing the time is "*no longer permitted* by us at all," which ultimately indicates our understanding of the "*overpowering nature*" of this boredom.[62] Heidegger contrasts between the first form of boredom, where we try to shout it down so that we do not have to listen to it, the second form, where we do not want to listen to it, and the profound form of boredom in which we are compelled to listen to it by what is authentic in our Da-sein in its ownmost freedom. This contrast is clearly reminiscent of the earlier inauthentic idle talk and call of conscience that compelled Da-sein to listen. I maintain that in the first two forms, there is an inauthentic covering up that attempts to silence the boredom, whereas in the profound form of boredom there is an authentic form of uncovering that silences Da-sein itself. Heidegger thus likens profound boredom to a "silent fog" that "draws back and forth . . . in the abysses of Dasein."[63] Such is the silencing force in the boredom that reveals itself "whenever we say or . . . silently know that *it is boring for one*." Moreover, Da-sein's silence here becomes more pervasive the deeper boredom draws it into its abysses, so that "the more profound the boredom, the more silent, the less public, the quieter, the more inconspicuous and wide-ranging it is."[64] Silently knowing and experiencing this form of boredom thus seem to involve a form of keeping silent and reticence as well. Moreover, Heidegger characterizes the time that stands in this form of boredom in terms of a "stillness" that spreads into Da-sein, wherein Da-sein scatters and hides itself.[65] The stillness in which Da-sein diffuses and conceals itself is thus the silent fog that reaches its abysses.

In profound boredom, the being left empty is characterized by an "indifference enveloping beings as a whole," as the indeterminate "it" and impersonal "one" reflect.[66] In Heidegger's rendition of this structural form, Da-sein is "*delivered over to beings' telling refusal as a whole*."[67] The telling refusal (*Versagen*) is thus a disclosure that is a telling (*Sagen*) in the manner of making manifest the possibilities of Da-sein in relation to beings as a whole that are denied or refused to it. This disclosure is thus also a telling announcement (*Ansagen*) that points to Da-sein's own "unexploited possibilities," like the earlier call of conscience in its appeal to Da-sein's potentiality-for-being. It discloses the self in its nullity as well, in that it "*brings* the *self* in all its nakedness *to itself* as the self that *is there*." Heidegger's depiction of the structural moment of being held in limbo here is also reminiscent of the compelling summons of the call of conscience in that Da-sein is "impelled" toward its possibilities in their "calling" (*Anrufen*).[68] The silencing that earlier unfolded through the call of care in Da-sein's temporality, as well as the earlier reticence of anticipatory resoluteness, now have their place in Da-sein's entrancement by time in profound boredom and in the moment of vision as the resolute self-disclosure.

The general correspondences mentioned above are also visible in Heidegger's depiction of our contemporary Da-sein in terms of a particular form of profound boredom. Thus, he claims that what "*announces and tells of itself*" in the telling refusal of today's essential oppressiveness "remains inaudible" and we remain "unable to hear" it. So, here he defines the task of metaphysics in the age of the profound boredom and silencing of the contemporary human in terms of helping "bring to word that which Da-sein wishes to speak about in this fundamental attunement—bring it to that word which is not simply a matter of gossip, but the word that addresses us and summons us to action and to being."[69]

At the same time, it is worth noting that, though the silencing that overpowers Da-sein and its corresponding hearkening and reticence in authenticity characterize both anxiety or dread and profound boredom, Heidegger distinguishes between what each mood discloses; dread or anxiety reveal (in *Being and Time*) the nullity of Da-sein's being or (in "What Is Metaphysics?") the nothing in its nihilating, while profound boredom reveals beings as a whole in their telling refusal, insofar as it "concerns beings as a whole and yet is not the Nothing."[70] In the end, both attunements are fundamental in defining Da-sein's being, and both the nihilating of the nothing and the telling refusal of beings as a whole reveal the being of beings in its withdrawal.

In conclusion, while Heidegger begins to view the problem of silence in terms of the truth of being, particularly in terms of its withdrawal, he still understands silence in terms of Da-sein's being and thereby remains at the pre-linguistic level. Moreover, in his analysis of profound boredom, he continues to define language in terms of the discourse that lets beings be seen as beings.[71] Thus, language still belongs fundamentally to Da-sein in its finitude and its world-forming essence. It belongs neither to immortals—for "to imagine a god expressing himself in speech is utterly meaningless"—nor to the animals, which are "poor in world" and have no access to beings as beings and are thus languageless.[72] In the next chapter, I will show how Heidegger takes the first step toward a primordial silence in his reflections on silence in relation to being itself at the same time that he places the human being within the essence of language and continues to exclude the gods and the animals.

NOTES

1. Martin Heidegger, *Being and Time*, trans. John Macquarrie and Edward Robinson (New York: Harper and Row, 1962), 298 / SZ, 222.
2. Ibid., 60 / SZ, 35.

3. Ibid., 227 / SZ, 161.
4. Ibid.
5. Ibid., 57 / SZ, 33. These possibilities of discourse would evidently also apply to the derivative mode of interpretation that takes form in the assertion or proposition (Cf. ibid., 293 / SZ, 218; 303 / SZ, 563).
6. Ibid., 298 / SZ, 222.
7. Ibid., 228–29 / SZ, 163.
8. Ibid., 56 / SZ, 33.
9. Ibid., 222 / SZ, 157. Emphasis added. Cf. ibid., 234 / SZ, 168.
10. Ibid., 221 / SZ, 296.
11. Ibid., 298 / SZ, 222.
12. Ibid., 235–37 / SZ, 169.
13. Ibid., 182 / SZ, 127.
14. Ibid., 238 / SZ, 170. Cf. ibid. 186 / SZ, 130.
15. Ibid., 365–66 / SZ, 276–77.
16. See ibid., 258 / SZ, 187; 336–40 / SZ, 253–56.
17. Ibid., 242 / SZ, 173.
18. Ibid., 389 / SZ, 296.
19. Ibid., 231 / SZ, 164.
20. Ibid., 358 / SZ, 271. Brandon Absher, "Speaking of Being: Language, Speech, and Silence in *Being and Time*" in *The Journal of Speculative Philosophy*, Vol. 30, Nr. 2 (2016): 204–31, appropriately characterizes idle talk as a "listening away from silence" (223).
21. See, for example, ibid., 298–99 / SZ, 222–23; 392 / SZ, 399.
22. Ibid., 231 / SZ, 165.
23. Ibid., 366 / SZ, 277.
24. Ibid., 389 / SZ, 296.
25. Ibid., 362 / SZ, 274.
26. Ibid., 402 / SZ, 305.
27. Ibid., 389 / SZ, 296.
28. Ibid., 362 / SZ, 274.
29. Ibid., 389 / SZ, 296.
30. Ibid., 363–66 / SZ, 275–78.
31. Ibid., 389 / SZ, 296.
32. Ibid., 362–66 / SZ, 274–77.
33. Ibid., 389 / SZ, 296.
34. See, ibid., 362 / SZ, 274.
35. Ibid., 259 / SZ, 188.
36. Ibid., 389 / SZ, 296.
37. Ibid. Absher, "Speaking of Being: Language, Speech, and Silence in *Being and Time*," seems to make similar claims, where authentic discourse is "a speaking grounded in silent listening to the ab-sent origin" (207) and the silent call of conscience reveals "the ab-sent self" (226).
38. Ibid., 262 / SZ, 190. It is worth recalling that Heidegger characterizes the they's inauthentic interpretation as providing a "protecting shelter" that hides

uncanniness (ibid., 238 / SZ, 170). However, this type of protective sheltering goes with the "tranquilization" that characterizes falling.

39. Ibid., 389–90 / SZ, 297.
40. Ibid., 395–96 / SZ, 301.
41. Ibid., 422–23 / SZ, 323.
42. Ibid., 497 / SZ, 383.
43. Ibid., 500 / SZ, 385.
44. Ibid., 259 / SZ, 187–88.
45. Heidegger, "What Is Metaphysics?," in *Pathmarks*, ed. William McNeill (Cambridge: Cambridge University Press, 1998), 90 / GA9, 114.
46. Ibid., 91–94 / GA9, 115–20.
47. Heidegger, *Being and Time*, 257 / SZ, 187.
48. Heidegger, "What Is Metaphysics?," 89 / GA9, 112.
49. Ibid., 90 / GA9, 114.
50. Ibid., 88 / GA9, 111–12.
51. Ibid., 91–92 / GA9, 115–16.
52. Ibid., 93 / GA9, 117.
53. Ibid., 89 / GA9, 112.
54. Ibid., 93 / GA9, 117–18.
55. Ibid., 86 / GA9, 109.
56. Ibid., 96 / GA9, 121–22.
57. Ibid., 93 / GA9, 118.
58. Ibid.
59. Ibid., 87 / GA9, 110.
60. Heidegger, *The Fundamental Concepts of Metaphysics: World, Finitude, Solitude*, trans. William McNeill and Nicholas Walker (Bloomington: Indiana University Press, 1995), 83 / GA29/30, 124.
61. Ibid., 127 / GA29/30, 191.
62. Ibid., 136 / GA29/30, 205.
63. Ibid., 80 / GA29/30, 119.
64. Ibid., 134 / GA29/30, 202.
65. Ibid., 122 / GA29/30, 183.
66. Ibid., 138 / GA29/30, 207.
67. Ibid., 139 / GA29/30, 208.
68. Ibid., 142–43 / GA29/30, 212–16.
69. Ibid., 164–67 / GA29/30, 245–49.
70. Ibid., 140 / GA29/30, 210.
71. Ibid., §72g.
72. Ibid., 238 / GA29/30, 346; §47.

Chapter 2

Toward the Essence of Silence

In the 1933–34 winter course "On the Essence of Truth," which Heidegger taught when he was rector of the University of Freiburg, he points to a decisive change in his conception of "keeping silent" (*schweigen*); in *Being and Time*, he viewed it as "an *ultimate* possibility of discourse," whereas, at this point, "discourse and language *arise from* keeping silent."[1] In section 2.1, I claim that this new meaning remains focused on Da-sein (human silence), so that it prepares for, but does not take the decisive step toward, the essence of silence as such in its relation to the unconcealedness of being. I will then prove in section 2.2 how the pivotal movement occurs instead when Heidegger begins his inquiry into the essence of language in the 1934 summer course, *Logic as the Question Concerning the Essence of Language*, which he taught shortly after his resignation as rector. It is at this point that he advances deeper into the pre-linguistic level and begins to ponder the primordial silence. I also argue that the political context of Heidegger's engagement with National Socialism during this short period cannot be ignored, not only because he brings it to bear in both lectures but also because it may have a bearing on what he says and does not say about silence.

2.1. ON THE ESSENCE OF TRUTH (1933–34)

Heidegger's approach to the question of truth and its essence had already undergone important shifts by the 1933–34 course. In his 1930 essay "On the Essence of Truth," he grounds Da-sein's freedom in the "more originary essence" of truth that he identifies as "the unconcealedness of beings-as-a-whole."[2] His 1931/32 essay "Plato's Doctrine of Truth" goes a step further by calling for the experience of "the 'positive' in the 'privative' essence of *alētheia*" as "the fundamental trait of being itself."[3] His detailed critique of Plato's transformation of truth into the "untruth" of the concept of correctness had also taken shape in the winter course of 1931–32, *The Essence of Truth. On Plato's Allegory of the Cave and Theaetetus*.[4] Though the 1933–34 course "On the Essence of Truth" repeats some of the content of this earlier course, there are significant differences, including a new introduction, "The Question of Essence as Insidious and Unavoidable," as well as the many fascist political interpretations charging Heidegger's discussion of the essence of truth. His re-articulation of the concept of keeping silent takes form in the new introduction, where it also takes on explicitly political meanings. A closer look at the context will reveal the significance of these changes.

Heidegger begins by assuming a layperson's perspective: It seems insidious to ask about the essence of truth, given the "urgency" of determining the "truth" and the "greatness" of the "fate" of the "German Dasein" to "*transform the spirit of world*." However, the layperson's perspective is inadequate, because to be true and to remain in the truth, we must first know what is truth and what distinguishes it from untruth; so, the question concerning the essence of truth is "unavoidable." Furthermore, the question concerning the "essence of essence" is also unavoidable. It is particularly pressing because the metaphysical definition of "essence" in terms of representation and concept has prevailed since the times of Plato.[5]

Heidegger proceeds to explain how "essence essences" in "our" Da-sein, through political concepts that are emblematic of the National Socialist ideology (the people, the state, labor). His explanation also involves recasting his earlier existential-ontological concepts (being-in-the-world, beings-as-a-whole, fundamental moods, and care) in explicit political terms. In this politically charged atmosphere, Heidegger calls for (what can be identified as) an authentic Da-sein, with the "originary courage" to grasp the essence of truth, proving "how much truth we can endure and withstand," and showing itself as what makes "Dasein sure, bright, and strong in its Being." Similarly, his signature being-question here inquires into what is essence. This inquiry must "hearken back" to "the Greek inception" as a matter of "the deepest necessity of our German Dasein," and it is "to draw on the fundamental possibilities of the Proto-Germanic ethnic essence and to bring these to mastery."[6]

Heidegger's interpretation of Heraclitus's concept of *polemos* as struggle or battle (*Kampf*) in the sense of "standing against the enemy," who can be "external" or "internal," speaks to the fascist politics of war and racist annihilation, though he explicitly disavows the "military" connotations. At the same time, it is evident that he aims to infuse distinctively philosophical meanings into the concept of struggle that are drawn from his thinking of truth as the unconcealedness of being in which the primordial struggle itself unfolds. Cast in Heidegger's terms, then, the Heraclitan struggle "pervades beings as a whole" in their "innermost necessity" through the "powers of generation and destruction" and "sets them into Being and holds them" in their "emergence" through "decision," "victory," and "defeat." The Heraclitan saying is thus itself at one and the same time a saying of "essence (being)" and of "*a-lētheia*," thought, not as correctness, but as "unconcealment."[7]

Heidegger advances from the hermeneutic circle concerning truth and essence in his interpretation of Heraclitus's saying to give words to his own saying. Claiming that we "always already fundamentally knew . . . in advance" what truth and the being of beings mean, he moves further onto his particular definition of the "*deepest*" human essence in terms of our "*bond to the superior power of Being*" insofar as we are "*transposed into*" and have in a way "*mastered*" it.[8] This characterization of being and beings as a whole in terms of "power" evidently blends with and, at the same time, imparts a philosophical sense to the political concept of the power of the German Dasein.

In his interpretation of Heraclitus's saying, Heidegger also outlines a concept of language that differs from its earlier definition (in *Being and Time*) as the worldly expressedness of discourse. Our understanding of words and of "the whole of language" is now ultimately based on the uniquely human essence of being transposed into and compelled by the superior power of being. Significantly, language is now the necessary medium of human existence: "Because and *only* because human beings are of this essence, they exist *in language*, and indeed there *must* be something like human *language*."[9] With this characterization of language, Heidegger opens the way for the (prelinguistic) question concerning its essence and its relation to the essence of truth as the unconcealedness of being.

Arguing that the metaphysical definitions of language (the logical-grammatical conception and its characterization as sign and expression) fail to capture its essence, Heidegger makes "only the most provisional remarks" with the aim of attaining its "positive delimitation."[10] Though he formulates many questions in this "provisional" endeavor and follows a few hermeneutical "circles," he does issue categorical answers to the question concerning the essence of language, as follows:

(1) The ability to keep silent is the origin and ground of language.
(2) Language is the gathered openness for the overpowering surge of beings.
(3) Language is the law-giving gathering and revelation of the structure of beings.

The focus of (1) and (2) remains on Da-sein's being in relation to the original meanings of *alētheia* as unconcealedness and *logos* as gathering, but with (3) being itself as presence (*parousia*) comes to the fore. I maintain that (1) and (2) remain focused on the existential phenomenon of silence, but the potential for reflection into its essence in relation to being lies unrealized in (3).

Turning our attention to Heidegger's discussion of keeping silent as the ground and origin of language, we find him leading his audience down various paths that he characterizes in terms of their circularity. However, some are more properly characterized as circuitous and even elusive. My sense is that this is because Heidegger's own keeping silent is at play in his discussion of keeping silent. The philosophical, political, and pedagogical reasons for his reticence could be said to mirror their interconnection in what he says about reticence as such.[11] In this manner, his audience—beginning with the German student in the fascist system of higher education—has to learn to discover what is not said but still shows itself and reveals its interconnected significance in his discussion of keeping silent and reticence.

The first problem Heidegger formulates in his discussion concerns the cogency of discussing the topic: If we talk about "keeping silent," then it seems that we know nothing about it. If we do not talk about it, then we may end up mystifying it. This superficial dilemma represents an inadequate approach to the topic, perhaps by a hypothetical layperson. However, Heidegger's reply does not address it directly or question its terms. Instead, he alludes to staying on the surface as well—he is not aiming for a "definition," but only for the "minimally necessary clarification" for pursuing the question concerning the essence of truth.[12]

The "clarification" seems to begin as Heidegger moves onto the second problem, which concerns the animal: Given that animals cannot speak because they are not bound to the superior power of being, one can infer that they have a higher capability for keeping silent than humans. This would contradict the assertion that language, which has its ground and origin in keeping silent, is unique to humans. Heidegger's response to this "remarkable and absurd" situation is that only the beings that are able to talk are able to keep silent. In particular, mutes differ fundamentally from windows and animals in their capacity for speech; the capacity or incapacity for vocalization does not define keeping silent. However, this response lands one in the "difficulty" of reversing the initial assertion by making the ability to talk the precondition for the ability to be silent. Heidegger seems to elude the issue by reaffirming the assertion that language arises from keeping silent. Moreover, though he has given much thought to the relationships between language and silence, he will "only communicate as is needed for the advancement of questioning."[13]

What Heidegger communicates is a deeper way of understanding keeping silent that reticently shows the inadequacy of the previous formulations at the same time that it explicitly averts other similarly misguided interpretations.

To keep silent, one must "have something to say," but this does not have the "simple" meaning that one must "*really* talk in the sense of speaking." Instead, it is in the "*exceptional*" sense that what one *has* to say, one has and keeps to oneself. This keeping to oneself, in turn, does not mean "being constrained, narrowness," but rather the "authentic" keeping to oneself that is "positive" as a being "opened up" to beings and to being in its superior power. This being "opened up," in turn, does not mean dispersing oneself by chasing after anything, but the "reverse" as "*the openness for beings that is gathered in itself.*" More precisely, "keeping silent" is "*the gathered disclosedness for the overpowering surge of beings as a whole.*"[14] In this sense, then, Heidegger is defining keeping silent in terms of Da-sein's truth in relation to *alētheia* as the truth of being in the unconcealment of beings. The gathering that characterizes Da-sein's openness and disclosedness, however, pertains to language as *logos* and *legein.* So, my claim is that he is hinting here at the essential relation of silence to truth and language in Da-sein's being.

Heidegger explicitly refers to language and discourse when he defines keeping silent as the "*happening* of the *originary reticence of human* Da-sein, a reticence by which Da-sein brings itself—that is, the whole of beings, in the midst of which it is—into words." With his definition of the word as the "binding formation" of gathered disclosedness and what it discloses, he implicitly refers to a function of *legein.* His characterization of the "word" and of "language" as what "*breaks silence*" encapsulates his assertion that language has its ground and origin in keeping silent and captures the disclosive power of language in relation to the truth of Da-sein's being. However, Heidegger's focus on reticence as an authentic fundamental mood narrows it down to a type of reticence that "gives voice to sound and vocalization" only in a word that "remains a true word," in a discourse that is not "mere idle talk" and does not pertain to the "*non-essence of language.*"[15]

Put otherwise, Heidegger conflates the essence of keeping silent with its authentic mode. At the same time that he claims that "keeping silent" is "the distinctive character of the Being of human beings," he distinguishes between the form of "non-essence," for example, by submission or evasion, and the form of essence that is "superiority, that is, power" as the "bound gathering of exposure."[16] It is only the authentic form of keeping silent, then, that he portrays as the origin and ground of language. This conflation of essence and authenticity can be seen in Heidegger's portrayal of "keeping silent" as "that power that both empowers vocalization into word and language and also empowers us to set ourselves against the superior power of Being and to maintain our position in it—and this means to speak and to be in language."[17] The specific political import of this portrayal is apparent given its context:

Heidegger reticently conveys the model of the authentic keeping silent of the German Dasein at the decisive moment of their fate.[18]

When Heidegger turns to the final consideration of the relation between the essence of truth as *alētheia* and the essence of language as *logos*, he makes use of Heraclitus's depiction of the *hoi polloi* to develop his own distinction between the authentic and inauthentic Da-sein in their manner of "being and discoursing." The "undisciplined masses" get "caught up in anything that is going on, disperse themselves in arbitrariness, and blather," that is, idle talk. Heidegger presents in contrast the model of authentic Da-sein as one who stands apart and in the "discipline of language."[19] Evidently, keeping silent is the fundamental mood of attunement for this paradigm that Heidegger suggests for the German Dasein.

At the same time, Heidegger's discussion of the ancient Greek interpretation of being as presence opens up the possibility for the move beyond his paradigmatic keeping silent toward the question concerning the essence of silence as such. It is in this context that he offers his second definition of language, this time, as the "lawgiving gathering and revelation of the structure of beings." This definition differs from the first (language as gathered openness for the overpowering surge of beings) in that it concerns language in its relation to beings as a whole. In this sense, Heidegger relates the Greek "essence of *logos*" as the "gathering" (*Sammlung*) that "enjoins beings" to the "essence of being" as the "co-presence" of beings. *Logos* as gathering is a revealing (*dēloun*) of beings. Therefore, it is essentially "a happening in which something previously inaccessible and veiled is torn from its concealment and set into un-concealment, *a-lētheia*, that is, truth."[20]

The essential relation between language as *logos* and truth as *alētheia* that Heidegger suggests here does not include a reference to silence as such. Is it, like keeping silent, the deeper ground and origin of language in Da-sein? Is it the ground and origin of the essence of language? Does the essence of language break this essential silence? How is silence as such related to truth as the unconcealedness of being? These are questions that Heidegger does not voice here, but most likely silently crossed his mind. However, a task that he sees as taking precedence is the inquiry into language in its relation to the being of beings. In his depiction, its accomplishment takes its own form of struggle in the confrontation with metaphysics and its logic. Thus, Heidegger proposes that for the question of the essence of language to be "at long last developed from the ground up," the "de-construction" of the grammatical-logical mode of thinking and representation and the "*destabilizing*" of the "*grammatical representation of language*" must occur.[21] As I will now show, he takes the first step in that direction in his 1934 summer course, *Logic as the Question Concerning the Essence of Language*.[22]

2.2. *LOGIC AS THE QUESTION CONCERNING THE ESSENCE OF LANGUAGE* (1934)

According to Günter Seubold (the editor of the original text), Heidegger changed the title of the 1934 summer course in question on the first day of class, from "The State and Science" to its present title. The fact that he had only recently resigned as rector has raised issues of whether the newly titled course reflects a change in his engagement and to what extent it represents his departure from the National Socialist state and ideological principles.[23] Even when one leaves aside his personal attitudes and motives, with the aim of focusing on the philosophical content of the course, it is impossible to ignore the political import that Heidegger himself makes explicit. At the same time, we would be remiss to overlook what is implicit and to remain deaf to what is unsaid in both its philosophical and political significance. This principle of interpretation is especially apposite to the question concerning the essence of silence, which Heidegger does not formulate at all in his stated project of "shaking up" logic as the question concerning the essence of language. A closer look into how this project unfolds will help to uncover the manifold importance of his silence about silence.

Heidegger's definition of the goal of shaking up logic as a "necessary task" is cast in the same warring terms used in the 1933–34 winter course "On the Essence of Truth." However, now the decisive "battle" or struggle (*Kampf*) for "our spiritual and historical destiny" is in the "confrontation" with the traditional logic of the propositional *logos.* The aim is to develop "a new logic" in a "creative overcoming, without which a transformation of our Da-sein will be baseless." This overcoming involves as well the creation of a "new form of discourse" against the "undisciplined idle talk" in traditional logic. Significantly, Heidegger depicts the task, which arises "out of the necessity of our fate" and is to be a "mandate for us," in terms of the being-question, directly as "the questioning pacing off abysses of being."[24] I claim that this formulation is key for perceiving the similar shift that occurs in his approach to the language-question.

As he begins to lay out the strategy for the battle over logic, Heidegger claims, "We cannot avoid the question concerning language and concerning the essence of language."[25] He does not explicitly dwell on the distinction that he makes between language and its essence in this claim. In addition, he seems to use the terms interchangeably in his lectures at times. However, as is well known, this distinction has been visible from early on—as in *Being and Time*, when he declared that the question of "what kind of Being goes with language in general" remained "open" after his inquiry into language as a phenomenon of Da-sein.[26] Now too, he concludes by denying that "we, after all, know what language is" and have reached the point of being able to "define the essence of language" with "the help of the gained insight into the . . . essence of Dasein."[27]

Yet, the crucial difference from earlier formulations is that now the question concerning the essence of language is "the fundamental and guiding question."[28] It takes the unique form of a "fore-question" as a question of essence, which "can never count as settled," as it is "constant[ly] . . . underway in the fore-field of the fore-questioning."[29] In fact, his answers to possible objections to defining the question concerning the essence of language as the directive and guiding principle for logic exclude metaphysical answers from the fore-field in advance. The "prejudice" and "error" of philosophies and sciences of language and its "preform[ation]" through propositional logic are canceled out as possible answers to the essence-question. In this sense, Heidegger pre-delineates what the essence of language is not: It is not a specific "area of objects," it is not merely a "secondary means of expression," and it is not reducible to "word-forms" and "grammatical" structures.[30] He later reinforces this pre-delineation with his rejection of metaphysical conceptions of language in terms of presence-at-hand (as what is preserved in the dictionary, as what happens when humans speak, and as an activity of the rational animal).[31]

Some of the questions that Heidegger includes in the fore-question in its threefold sense (as questioning ahead, questioning forward, and preceding) speak directly to the distinction between language and its essence, for example, "What kind of being [*Art zu sein*] does a language have? Is there in general something like language in general?" Some also suggest answers that point toward the essence of language, for example, "What is the ground of possibility? Where does this ground [*Grund*] become an abyss [*Abgrund*]?"[32] The latter example is particularly noteworthy because it is reflected in the first circle that Heidegger draws in the mutual definition of "the being and essence of language," which is "dark and enigmatic," and the being of the human being. Staying in the circle, rather than evading it, we find that the "circling" "gradually becomes a vortex" and this "vortex draw us slowly into an abyss." However, instead of explicitly plunging into this abyss as one that belongs to being itself in relation to the essence of language, he first follows the direction of the circle toward the essence of the human being.[33]

In his approach to the language-question through the Dasein-question, Heidegger once again politicizes philosophical concepts and endows political concepts with philosophical meaning. The question concerning human essence thus becomes a matter of the resoluteness and the decisive being-historical of the *Volk*. Having reached the definition of human essence in Da-sein's temporalizing of time and its transformation through the responsibility (*Verantwortung*) that answers to (*Antworten*) and answers for (*Verantworten*) history, Heidegger averts the "misunderstanding" of the decision-like questioning and answering as a "politics of the day position," instead of the "awakening of an original knowing" in Da-sein.[34] However, my sense is that this proviso does not alter the political nature of the awakening when he renders it in his philosophical terms. To this effect, the reversal of the question-sequence, from the original time back to the essence of language, leads us back to the mood, labor, mission, and mandate of the *Volk* and the State as its historical being and as the historical power jointure empowered by Da-sein's care of freedom.

Heidegger defines language at the end of the inquiry into the essence of language in terms that pertain specifically to "the *Volk*": It is "the ruling of the world-forming and preserving center" of its "historical *Dasein*."[35] Cast in terms of the German Dasein, this definition echoes the political tone of the entire question-sequence and speaks to the fascist politics of the time. However, I maintain that at the same time it advances deeper into the pre-linguistic level in that it also points to the *essence* of language, which remains undefined, "continuously" and "always already" in the inquiry, though "not explicitly" and "not transparent to us." Heidegger hints at this essence as he links language to being and to truth, which he understands here as "the manifestness of beings" that "fits and binds us into the being of beings."[36] Language is the ruling of the "world-forming and preserving center" insofar as we are "exposed in the manifest beings and . . . time," which means that "the being of beings is transferred to us" and that being "as a whole, as it rules through and rules around us . . . is the *world*." More directly, he claims here that "the essence of language essences where it happens as world-forming power."[37]

I maintain that Heidegger takes a decisive step toward the essence of language with the suggestion that it essences and happens as a disclosive and shaping force of the being of beings. However, he also remains entrenched in the specific role of language in relation to the *Volk*, particularly as the "preserving" center of its historical being. Such preservation takes place in lore (*Kunde*), in which world announces (*kündet*) itself and through which world rules. In this sense, it is "in the primal-event of language" that lore happens.[38] Language in its relation to the historical being of the *Volk* is the primordial happening in which lore itself happens, is manifested (*bekundet*), and is deliberately (in knowing and willing) preserved, so that it remains explorable (*erkundbar*).[39]

Heidegger's idea of language in relation to lore has a dynamic and positive sense that contrasts with the *Being and Time* definition of language as the worldly expressedness of discourse that in its everydayness takes the form of idle talk. Another important factor in the relation between language and lore is the positive concept of tradition (*Überlieferung*) as the "innermost character of our historicity," through which "our own determination is carried off over [*über*] ourselves," and through it "we are delivered [*ausgeliefert*] into the future."[40] Tradition thus conceived ultimately serves as the basis for Heidegger's model of the *Volk* in the "resoluteness" of its historical Dasein.[41] Da-sein has the possibility to "take over [*übernehmen*]" and subordinate itself to tradition.[42] Additionally, according to Heidegger's prescription, tradition "is to be appropriated only *in such a manner* that we expressly take it over and are in it *itself*."[43]

The language in which lore happens is the language in which tradition is preserved and can be resolutely taken over in Da-sein's "historical being as futurality, as care."[44] Heidegger sees in this language the ground of the possibility for an authentic form of discourse. What is remarkable is that, insofar as it is the language and discourse of the *Volk*, this suggests that he is exploring a positive sense of its *everydayness* that is not that of the inauthentic idle talk. It is thus significant that he does not explicitly (re)introduce his earlier concept of the authentic keeping silent and reticence as the fundamental mood of the *Volk*. However, he emphasizes instead that it is from the language of poetry as the "original language" that "the Germans, who talk so much about discipline [*Zucht*], must learn what it means to preserve that which they already possess."[45] So, while the language in which lore happens and in which tradition delivers Da-sein to its future is the language of the *Volk*, it is in poetry that its authentic possibilities lie. I believe that it is evident that the discipline that is required for learning and that is modeled in the true poets includes hearkening, keeping silent, and reticence.

Heidegger makes only three explicit references to silence. In one of these references, he contrasts the "great mood" of the *Volk*, which may be "silent in the great work," with the noisy "small mood," which "continually displays itself, be it in wretchedness or dull boisterousness."[46] In the other two references, he poses preliminary questions concerning language: "Is language only then, when it is spoken? Is it not, when one is silent?" and "Does it cease to be, if one is silent?"[47] However, I maintain that the clue to a deeper meaning of silence lies in his discussion of what lies concealed in lore. Lore announces "beings," but the "genuine lore of history announces . . . precisely as it sets us before that which is concealed," so that the "mystery of the moment" is "the lore of that which is overpowering and inevitable."[48] In this sense, I claim that the primordial silence is at play in lore, for we can infer that, while lore announces beings (what is unconcealed), it *silently* sets us before the being of beings in its concealedness. As Heidegger puts it, lore "is the manifestness of the being of beings in the mystery."[49]

Furthermore, I claim that, insofar as lore happens in language, the clue to the primeval meaning of silence in relation to being and its mystery also lies in language. In language, "the exposedness into beings, the delivering over

[*Überantwortung*] to being happens," and it "is nothing other than the event of the exposedness entrusted [*überantworteten*] to being into beings as a whole."[50] In this light, I claim that, in its disclosive essence, language silently delivers Da-sein over to being in its concealedness and mystery as well. In this sense, Heidegger's approach to language in its essence suggests a more original silence that is not the silence of Da-sein, but the primeval silence of being.

Heidegger's characterization of language in its essence as the ruling of the world-forming power also suggests that the possibilities of speech and silence, as well as their distinctions in terms of authenticity and inauthenticity, are defined for Da-sein in its historical being. As the "original language," the language of poetry is where "the essence of language essences," where "it happens as world-forming power."[51] Thus, I maintain that this primordial historical happening unfolds silently while it empowers language as disclosive word and Da-sein itself in its exposedness to beings in their being. Heidegger links poetry with "the proper language," that is, with an authentic world-forming power, and claims that these "happen only where the ruling of being is brought into the superior untouchability of the original word."[52] It follows that this original word belongs to being and that its superior untouchability reflects the depth of its silence, the extent of its concealedness.

Heidegger singles out the authentic or "true" poetry as "the language of that being [*Sein*] that was forespoken to us a long time already and that we have never before caught up with."[53] In their attunement to the essence of language, the true poets would thus be among those who experience what Heidegger calls "the great fundamental moods," which "the more powerful they are, the more concealed they work."[54] Presumably, these great moods would also work in "great thinkers," in the likes of Heraclitus and Parmenides.[55] They would also work in those whose philosophizing drives them to the fore-field of the fore-questions and "thereby always touch at something great within the *Dasein* of the human being."[56] It would follow that the more powerful the attunement of great thinkers and true poets to the essence of language, the more reticently they would speak. In the next chapter, we will see how Heidegger's 1935 winter course on Hölderlin's Hymns "Germania" and "The Rhein" is another reticent effort to inquire into the essence of silence, this time through a dialogue with the poet of poets.

NOTES

1. Martin Heidegger, "On the Essence of Truth," in *Being and Truth*, trans. Gregory Fried and Richard Polt (Indiana: Indiana University Press: 2010), 86 / GA36/37, 107.

2. Heidegger, "On the Essence of Truth," in *Pathmarks*, trans. William McNeill (Cambridge: Cambridge University Press, 1998), 142–44 / GA9, 185–87. Cf. ibid., 153–54 / GA9, 201–02.

3. Heidegger, "Plato's Doctrine of Truth," in *Pathmarks*, 179 / GA9, 233.

4. Heidegger, *The Essence of Truth. On Plato's Allegory of the Cave and Theaetetus*, trans. Ted Sadler (London: Continuum, 2002) / GA34.

5. Heidegger, "On the Essence of Truth," in *Being and Truth*, 67–69 / GA36/37, 83–86.

6. Ibid., §2b.

7. Ibid., §3a–§3b; §4a.

8. Ibid., 80 / GA36/37, 100.

9. Ibid., 80 / GA36/37, 100–01. A similar characterization can be found in "The Fundamental Questions of Philosophy," in *Being and Truth*, where it is "in" language as the "dominant fundamental reality of . . . being-with-one-another," that the individual is defined on the "basis of the shared world and spiritual community" (ibid., 46 / GA36/37, 57–58).

10. Ibid., 81 / GA36/37, 101; and §5d.

11. Heidegger's private notes on the importance of being reticent and bearing silence during the period of 1931–35 could be interpreted in these three senses. See especially, Heidegger, in *Ponderings II–VI: Black Notebooks 1931–1938*, trans. Richard Roczewicz (Bloomington and Indianapolis: Indiana University Press, 2016).

12. Heidegger, "On the Essence of Truth," in *Being and Truth,* 85 / GA36/37, 107.

13. Ibid., 87 / GA36/37, 110.

14. Ibid., 87 / GA36/37, 111.

15. Ibid., 88–89 / GA36/37, 112.

16. Ibid., 88 / GA36/37, 112. Compare with "The Fundamental Questions of Philosophy," where it is "in language" where "beings as a whole reveal themselves according to the powers that hold sway in them," insofar as it is what "preserves and increases the world into which a people exists in every case" (ibid., 46 / GA36/37, 58).

17. Ibid. Bernard, P. Dauenhauer, *Silence: The Phenomenon and its Ontological Significance* (Bloomington, Indiana: Indiana University Press, 1980) seems to be expressing the same point when he argues that *Being and Time* restricts silence to the mode of authentic discourse rather than to discourse itself (chapter 5).

18. In one of his later private notes, Heidegger makes explicit the connection between Hölderlin as the founder of the "German future," and the "futural Germans" in the age of the "noise" of machination, whose "future—as German—will become a long struggle in which many will fall in silent reticence." Heidegger, *Ponderings VII-XII: Black Notebooks 1938–1939,* trans. Richard Rojcewicz (Bloomington and Indianapolis: Indiana University Press, 2017), 154 / GA94 VII-XII, 198.

19. Heidegger, "On the Essence of Truth," in *Being and Truth*, 91 / GA36/37, 115.

20. Ibid., 91 / GA36/37, 115–16.

21. Ibid., 82 / GA36/37, 104.

22. Heidegger himself identifies this seminar as his first step in that direction. See: Heidegger, "A Dialogue on Language," in *On the Way to Language*, trans. Peter D. Hertz (New York: Harper & Row, 1971), 8 / US, 93–94; and Heidegger, *What Is Called Thinking?*, trans. J. Glenn Gray (New York: Harper and Row, 1968), 154 / GA8, 100.

23. Günter Seubold, "Editor's Epilogue" in Heidegger, *Logic as the Question Concerning the Essence of Language*, trans. Wanda Torres Gregory and Yvonne Unna (Albany, New York: State University of New York Press, 2010),144 / GA38, 172. One of the most recent contributions to this particular issue is Adam Knowles, *Heidegger's Fascist Affinities: A Politics of Silence* (Stanford, California: Stanford University Press, 2019), especially chapters 1 and 2.

24. Heidegger, *Logic as the Question Concerning the Essence of Language*, 8 / GA38, 9–10.

25. Ibid., 11 / GA38, 13.

26. Heidegger, *Being and Time*, 209–10 / SZ, 155.

27. Heidegger, *Logic as the Question Concerning the Essence of Language*, 139 / GA38, 167.

28. Ibid., 11 / GA38, 13.

29. Ibid., 19 / GA38, 22.

30. Ibid., §5.

31. Ibid., §7–§8.

32. Ibid., 16 / GA38, 19.

33. Ibid., §8.

34. Ibid., 101 / GA38, 122.

35. Ibid., 140 / GA38, 169.

36. Ibid., 67–68 / GA38, 78–79. Cf. ibid., 140, GA38, 168.

37. Ibid., 141 / GA38, 170.

38. Ibid., 140–41 / GA38, 168–70.

39. Ibid., 73–74 / GA38, 86–87.

40. Ibid., 98 / GA38, 117–18.

41. See especially ibid., §28c.

42. Ibid., 100 / GA38, 120.

43. Ibid., 104 / GA38, 125.

44. Ibid., 137 / GA38, 166.

45. Ibid., 141–42 / GA38, 170. For a similar connection between the language of tradition and poetry in later years (1962), see Heidegger, "Traditional Language and Technological Language" trans. Wanda Torres Gregory, *Journal of Philosophical Research*, Vol. XXIII (1998): 129–45 / UT.

46. Ibid., 108 / GA38, 129–30.

47. Cf. ibid., 22 / GA38, 24; 29 / GA38, 31.

48. Ibid., 131–32 / GA38, 159–60.

49. Ibid., 140 / GA38, 168.

50. Ibid.

51. Ibid., 141 / GA38, 170.

52. Ibid., 142 / GA38, 170.

53. Ibid., 141–42 / GA38, 170.
54. Ibid., 108 / GA38, 130.
55. Ibid., 93 / GA38, 111–12.
56. Ibid., 19 / GA38, 22.

Chapter 3

The Poetics of Silence in a Dialogue with Hölderlin

Heidegger's 1934–35 interpretation of Hölderlin in *Hölderlin's Hymns "Germania" and "The Rhein"* centers on Hölderlin's poetry as the inaugural saying that reticently founds and projects the German Dasein. I maintain that Heidegger advances his own reflections on silence and language in relation to beyng in his reading of the poems. My contention is specifically that, through his dialogue with the poet of poets and of poetizing, he develops his definition of (primordial) silence as the origin of language, as well as his definition of language as the originary site of the unconcealedness of beyng, which pertains to what I identify as the primeval silence. Correspondingly, Heidegger characterizes authentic hearkening and reticence in terms of their attunement to the mystery of beyng in its concealedness. Taken together, these points corroborate my working thesis for this period concerning the continual links between his evolving concepts of silence, language, and truth. I will discuss how these connections appear as Heidegger gives voice to his own poetics of silence in his interpretation of "Germania" in section 3.1 and turn to "The Rhein" in section 3.2.

3.1. GERMANIA

Heidegger's thoughts on silence are insinuated from the start, in the Preliminary Remark that calls for a long "silence" concerning Hölderlin, especially given that he is in vogue.[1] Heidegger thereby suggests that his objective is to maintain the silence around Hölderlin, even as he would appear to be breaking the silence in his own elucidations. After all, as he later admits, it is "inevitable" that we must talk about Hölderlin and his poetic works. However, Heidegger also suggests here that the important point is *how* this is done, in a "*thoughtful* encounter" with the "*revelation of beyng*" attained in his poetry.[2] I maintain that Heidegger is reticently hinting that his thoughtful words about the poet are *themselves* reticent—intimating and leaving unsaid what is unsayable and what cannot be said concerning its revelation of beyng now. Thus, in the conclusion to his reading of "Germania," he portrays himself as the thinker engaged in a dialogue that shelters the poet in the reticence of his thinking.[3] Still, Heidegger manages to make his own thinking manifest in his interpretation of Hölderlin.

In Heidegger's rendition, the poet's work in its essential aspect plays the role of grounding the "commencement of another history," which begins with the struggle over the decision concerning the gods in their flight or arrival.[4] In this light, he claims that Hölderlin is himself reticent as he points to this commencement or origin in the poem "Germania." One of Hölderlin's later fragments offers an essential clue to his reticence, which is epitomized in the verse "Concerning what is highest, I shall be silent." Heidegger's interpretation links the concealed origin of the German fatherland as the "origin withheld in silence" with the poet's reticent grounding. Given the constant "danger" of the inauthentic approach to poetry, Heidegger calls for the propaedeutic that will keep us on the path of the poetics of silence. This is the explicit role of the preparatory reflection on poetry and language that follows, namely, to anchor what we know about and experience in the poetizing, thinking, and saying of the historical Da-sein.[5] At the same time, it will be through his reading of the poet's words that he reticently gives voice to his thoughts on silence and language in relation to the unconcealedness of beyng.

Heidegger's characterization of poetizing as a telling or saying (*sagen*) that makes manifest in the manner of pointing emphasizes the disclosive power of poetry in its grounding of beyng. The experience of this power "thrusts" us out of everydayness, which is the domain from which poetry itself is "expelled."[6] Everydayness is the veritable counter-domain of poetry, where a poem is merely a present-at-hand thing that we read and listen to, instead of a force in which the "overarching resonance . . . oscillates in the word." Heidegger suggests here that it is precisely in the everyday understanding of language as an instrument of communication that a poem can appear denuded of its revelatory force, that is, of its disclosive power.[7]

Heidegger appears to reverse the instrumental interpretation of language: "It is not we who have language; rather, language has us, in a certain way."[8] I maintain that this apparent reversal is instead an attempt to overcome the metaphysical view through which he reticently points to language as belonging to the truth of beyng. Heidegger's intimation becomes more evident as he reflects on Hölderlin's depiction of language as "the most dangerous of goods." Ignoring the instrumental connotations of language as a good that we possess as gifts from the gods, Heidegger focuses on the dangerousness of language, which he identifies as the site of unconcealedness, the "originary unveiling itself," which is thus also a "veiling" and "*semblance*."[9] I claim that this identification tightens the link between language as the showing or revelation of beings and truth as the unconcealedness of being. In this sense, it brings us closer to the primeval silence.

Hölderlin's poetic verse "Since we are a dialogue" serves as a springboard for Heidegger's reformulation of the earlier talking-with-one-another of being-in-the-world. Now, it is couched in terms of the determination of our being by language as an event or happening of language (*Sprachgeschehnis*) itself.[10] This disclosive event that occurs temporally and grounds our historical beyng enables the disclosive possibilities of our saying as forms of unveiling and veiling in language.[11]

In his interpretation of Hölderlin's poetic image of humans as a dialogue, Heidegger assigns different meanings to the dialogue that we are, as follows:

(1) The primordial dialogue in which the gods (a) address us or (b) don't address us.
(2) The commencing dialogue of poetizing.
(3) The dialogue that we are as a keeping silent, which is essentially linked to our being able to hear, which, in turn, is equiprimordial with saying.
(4) The dialogue that we are as idle talk, which is the necessary unessence or non-essence of dialogue, and is thus part of the danger that comes from language. In fact, it plays an essential role in the danger because language essentially contains its own decline.[12]

However, Heidegger also depicts idle talk as one of the two options facing the German Dasein at the historical moment of its decision regarding their identity as dialogue or as idle talk.[13] In this sense, he continues to leave open the possibility for the *Volk* as a community to be an authentic dialogue, but there are strict requirements. The individual must first be "exposed in advance" to beings, which "occurs through language, as the originary founding of beyng."[14] This originary founding enables the hearing from, being with, and being for one another that forms a community.[15] However, the ability to hear can take on an inauthentic form, as an "essential mishearing" in which we can miss what is being talked about or to whom the talking is addressed.[16]

In three of the four meanings of the dialogue that we are, we can find a particular type of silence, as follows:

(1) In the primordial dialogue in which the gods (a) address us or (b) don't address us, the gods themselves are silent in the sense that they do not speak in word-sounds.

a) When the gods do address us, they beckon.[17] Claiming that Heraclitus had a decisive influence in Hölderlin, Heidegger draws from Heraclitus's statement on the god Apollo, who "neither conceals nor reveals, but beckons." Accordingly, he renders their beckoning as an "originary saying" that points.[18]
b) When the gods don't address us, there is not even a silent beckoning, though the silence of the gods makes something manifest in the very absence of their beckoning. The "holy mourning" that Heidegger interprets in Hölderlin's poetry is the fundamental attunement to this case, specifically with regard to the gods in their flight.[19]

(2) It is in poetizing that the gods' beckoning is "shrouded in the word," and thereby in the "*originary language of a people.*" In some of Hölderlin's poems and fragments, the language of the gods is the language of thunderstorms and lightning.[20] However, in the poem "Germania," the eagle serves as the messenger of the gods and is able to speak in word-sounds with the man and the girl (whom Heidegger identifies as Germania). In Heidegger's interpretation, all those named in the poem, including the eagle, speak of language in a naming that yet leaves it unspoken. In this sense, their dialogue "brings language to language."[21] Thus, Hölderlin's poems exemplify the commencing dialogue of poetizing. Moreover, his poems not only speak of reticence (the solitary speech full of golden words and the call to leave something unspoken in naming) but are also reticent in themselves.

(3) Keeping silent (*erschweigen*) is the authentic form of silence (*Schweigen*) in the dialogue that we are. In this sense, Heidegger's earlier tendency to conflate essence with authenticity with regard to keeping silence continues. He claims here that keeping silent and the ability to talk are "essentially unified." In this context, he seems to be referring to the broad sense of being able to talk, that is, as the ability to speak in word-sounds, for he excludes people who are born mute when he proclaims, "Only whoever can keep silent can also talk."[22] The poetic and thoughtful telling are the models of keeping silent (and thus of saying and talking). The poetic telling, which Hölderlin's poetry exemplifies, keeps silent insofar as it leaves "the unsayable unsaid" and does so "in and through its telling."[23] To illustrate the thoughtful telling, Heidegger offers the (most likely, self-referential) example of a genuine philosophical lecture, in which what is most important is kept silent.[24]

Heidegger's contrast between the dialogue that we are as a keeping silent (3) and as an idle talk (4) focuses on the originary and authentic telling that is exemplified in the poetic founding—the "'first-born' of language," and the "fateful necessity of a decline," in which it becomes "leveled off" in the inauthentic realm. In his depiction here, idle talk is not disclosive, insofar as it only appears to say and thus to show beings. So, Heidegger suggests in this context that, as the "fallen version" of poetic saying, idle talk is *incapable* of keeping silent, that is, of the silence of the authentic saying.[25] It is thereby a way of talking everything to death to which we become enslaved. Thus, he admonishes that "one cannot simply ramble on," if one is "to simultaneously preserve in silence what is essential to one's saying."[26]

In conclusion, Heidegger's interpretation of "Germania" does not explicitly refer to a silence that is deeper than Da-sein's keeping silent and even deeper than the beckoning of the gods in Hölderlin's poetry. However, I maintain that his definition of language as the primordial site of unconcealedness and as the event that defines Da-sein's historical beyng points to beyng in its concealedness, and this concealedness lies in a primeval silence. I also claim that we are entering the proto-linguistic level, for by virtue of its role as the site of the "originary unveiling" of beyng itself, language is *itself* determined by the originary concealedness of beyng.[27] Heidegger's characterization of language as the site of the "confrontational setting-apart [*Aus-einander-setzung*] of beyng and non-being" suggests as much.[28] In the end, it is in the wresting away from the originary concealedness of beyng into its unconcealedness in beings that this confrontational setting-apart unfolds. Put otherwise, language is grounded in the essence of truth and has its origin in what Heidegger will later identify as the stillness. That said, here, he explicitly circumscribes his intimation of the primeval silence in his characterization of the essence of truth as the "manifestness of beings." The concealing and veiling are themselves a form of manifestness and this indicates that mystery is the "highest figure of truth."[29] However, instead of delving into the mystery as it relates to language as such, Heidegger focuses on its authentic poetic saying as "*denial*," which in its reticence makes the mystery manifest as such, while at the same time leaving its "concealing power" untouched (just as he silently does in his own focus).[30] Heidegger also refers to the "originary origin of language" the grounds Da-sein as a "mystery."[31] Once again, he leaves the mystery as it relates to language untouched. However, the concealing and veiling character of the mystery intimates to silence as that originary origin, which I maintain is the primeval silence.

3.2. THE RHEIN

My position is that it is in the interpretation of "The Rhein" where Heidegger offers more hints regarding the mystery and explicitly reflects on the primeval silence that is itself the origin of language. It is worth noting, however, that the primordial silence of language in its essence is not a topic here either.

Focusing first on his explicit reflection, we find him returning to Hölderlin's depiction of language as the most dangerous of goods as meaning that in language beyng "first opens itself up" to us and thereby "transports" us into the realm of the general "threatening" of beyng. With language as the primordial site of the *un*concealedness of beyng *itself,* Heidegger continues to take the decisive steps in the same direction that he took in his interpretation of "Germania." However, now he goes deeper into the origin of language and identifies it as the silence that precedes the world and is "more powerful" than all our powers. With its origin in the silence from which beyng unconceals itself and which precedes the disclosive whole that is the world, language is thus the abode into which humans are thrown into the dialogue that we are. It is worth noting in this regard that Heidegger here characterizes human silence as a possibility that has to be wrested away "in drawing back" from the discourse that is always already expressed. In this sense, Heidegger continues to interpret the Hölderlinian dialogue in terms of the extremes between idle talk and the reticent saying of poetry and thinking. At one extreme, we find the dangerous inauthentic discourse, in which language focuses on what is said and thereby dwindles into idle talk. At the other extreme lies the poetic "originary telling," but as the "originary language of a people," which declines in its dissemination as prose.[32]

I maintain that Heidegger links mystery in general, which suggests the primeval silence, with the poet's reticence as co-responding to the mystery's veiling character at the same time that he unveils it in his poem. One instance in which Heidegger develops this connection is inspired in the fourth strophe (IV, 73) of "Germania," which begins thus: "Enigma is that which has purely sprung forth. Even / The song may scarcely unveil it."[33] In Heidegger's interpretation, the task of the poet is "to unveil the mystery of beyng." Yet, what defines the "great and genuine" poetizing here is that it will "necessarily fall short" in its endeavor. I claim that this falling short means that it is *silenced* in its unveiling. Heidegger thus highlights the limits of the song, which "may scarcely unveil the mystery," and he interprets these as the limits imposed on poetic saying by what is unsayable.[34] Therefore, this is the silence that is imposed upon saying in the refusal of beyng itself, in its withdrawal into its deepest concealedness in the mystery.[35]

I claim that the silence that takes form in the poet's reticence can be related to what Heidegger describes as understanding "authentically," which is tantamount to "knowledge of the inexplicable" that "precisely lets what is inexplicable stand as such."[36] In this manner, poetizing still unveils the mystery *as* mystery in its song, bringing us "thereby first face-to-face with the full mystery."[37] Thus, with regard to understanding an enigma, Heidegger claims that the "more originarily we understand, the further that which is unexplained and inexplicable is unveiled."[38] Arguing that "intimacy" (*Innigkeit*) is a foundational word in Hölderlin that names the mystery belonging to the beyng that has sprung forth, Heidegger again portrays the poetic naming, the "unveiling" of the mystery in terms that suggest its profound reticence, as "a not wanting to explain, but rather understanding it as self-concealing concealment."[39] In its fundamental attunement with the intimacy of beyng, poetizing is thus "always an intimating" (*Ahnen*), that is, a reticent hinting.[40] In this sense, Heidegger says that the poetizing song is "more a telling that veils than one that unveils."[41] The reticent poetic saying of the mystery, which is the originary language of a people, shelters the mystery in silence. In this manner, the saying stands "unsaid among the people." Yet, even as this language declines into idle talk, into what Heidegger refers to as the language that is merely a "shell of communication and veiling," the saying remains "in what is concealed."[42]

Heidegger ascribes a special kind of hearing that essentially accompanies the poetic saying—the "originary" hearing, which he distinguishes from "customary" forms of hearing.[43] The latter forms of hearing include, not only acoustical experiences, such as hearing the sound of bells that penetrates our ears, but also attitudes with regard to hearing, such as listening out for something in our curiosity or being immersed in and captivated by what is heard. The more important distinction between the poetic and two other forms of hearing, one belonging to the gods and the other belonging to mortals, is inspired mainly by the second strophe of "The Rhein." In Heidegger's interpretation, the poet's hearing is captured in the stanza "I heard him pining for deliverance," the gods' hearing is that of pity, and the mortals' hearing is one of fleeing. The pity of the gods takes the form of an acquiescent hearing (*Erhören*), while the fleeing form of hearing of mortals is "a *failure to hear* [Überhören] and an unwillingness to hear."[44] I believe that this is patently the inauthentic hearing that accompanies idle talk and that in its flight from the mysterious origin of beyng loudly makes manifest its horror of silence.

The poet differs from the gods, who simply let the origin go, and from the mortals who flee from it, in that the poet "stands firm" before it. This poetic hearing that stands firm evidently involves a keeping silent as well as an anticipatory readiness, which Heidegger characterizes in terms of its being a hearing that "discerns in advance."[45]As the demigod who stands in the middle of beyng, between the gods and the mortals, as an overhuman and an undergod, whose hearing neither pities nor flees, the poet hears in the manner of an "originary apprehending" of the origin as such.[46]

What the poet hears, according to Heidegger's interpretation, is the springing forth of language from its origin, that is, from what I identify as the primeval silence of beyng in its supreme concealedness. It is a "fettered" origin precisely because of this concealedness. In this vein, Heidegger claims that the poet's hearing is one that "partakes in and lets resonate the leap [*Sprung*]."[47] This leap is that of the origin (*Ursprung*), in front of which the poet stands firm. In this leap of the origin, beyng unconceals itself in the language of the people through the poet's founding word. In his originary hearing, the poet lets this silence resound, by corresponding to it in his sonorous saying. The poetic saying is thereby the originary language of the people in the dialogue that we are. At the same time, the poet's sounding of the word keeps silent in the manner of sheltering the primeval silence insofar as the "word shelters within it the truth concerning the originary origin."[48]

Speaking of the demigods, Heidegger claims that the mystery of their beyng is "essentially concealed."[49] Those who will find it most difficult to grasp and to retain are evidently the inauthentic mortals in their idle talk, hearing that flees, and horror of silence. However, Heidegger envisions the possibility of poetry (in fact, he cherishes the hope) that the poetizing word will induce the mortals to face the mystery as it becomes "uncircumventable" for those who refuse to hear, so that they are ultimately compelled to listen to it.[50] Thus, in spite of the challenges that the mystery poses for the inauthentic humans, the retaining, which involves the reticent sheltering of the mystery in the poem, serves the higher purpose of the self-determination of their historical Da-sein within beyng.[51]

In his interpretation of both "Germania" and "The Rhein," Heidegger explicitly identifies Hölderlin as the poet who is at the same time the thinker or the thinker-poet. He distinguishes poetic from everyday thinking as well.[52] He also takes pains to distinguish it from and avert its misinterpretation in terms of the traditional thinking of metaphysics.[53] At the same time, poetic and (genuine) philosophical thinking both remain "fundamentally different" from the everyday thinking.[54] The difference between the two forms of authentic thinking themselves is much subtler, but still visible in Heidegger's characterization of Hölderlin's *poetic* thinking and saying as a "founding" projection, instead of one that grasps beyng as a concept.[55] Heidegger also portrays his own aim as a "thoughtful and philosophical endeavor to empower the power of the essence of poetry."[56] In particular, he marks the recognition of silence as the origin of language as a *philosophical* moment of reflection.[57] As I hope to have shown, Heidegger nonetheless manages to give reticent expression to his own thoughts in the poetics of silence. My conclusion is that he thereby moves closer to the primeval silence as he draws closer links between silence, language, and truth in relation to beyng. In the next chapter, we witness how he begins to make these thoughts manifest in his private manuscript from 1936 to 1938 in which he focuses on the event (*Ereignis*).

NOTES

1. Martin Heidegger, *Hölderlin's Hymns "Germania" and "The Rhein,"* trans. William McNeill and Julia Anne Ireland (Indiana: Indiana University Press, 2014), 2 / GA39, 1.
2. Ibid., 4–5 / GA39, 4–6.
3. Ibid., 132 / GA39, 151.
4. Ibid., 2 / GA39, 1.
5. Ibid., 4–5 / GA39, 4–6.
6. For examples, see ibid., 21–26 / GA39, 20–26.
7. Ibid., 24 / GA39, 23.
8. Ibid. See also, ibid., 60–61 / GA39, 66; 67 / GA39, 74.
9. Ibid., 57–58 / GA39, 61–62. See also, ibid., 64 / GA39, 70.
10. See, ibid., §7e–§7i.
11. Ibid., 64 / GA39, 70.
12. Ibid., 63–67 / GA39, 70–74.
13. Ibid., 69–70 / GA39, 77.
14. Ibid., 66 / GA39, 73. See section 2.1 for my discussion of his earlier idea of the authentic discourse and silence of the *Volk* in *Logic as the Question Concerning the Essence of Language*.
15. Ibid., 66–67 / GA39, 73.
16. Ibid., 40 / GA39, 41.
17. Ibid., 31 / GA39, 32.
18. Ibid., 114 / GA39, 127.
19. Ibid., Chapter Two; §8.
20. Cf. ibid., 30–31 / GA39, 31–32; 59 / GA39, 64.
21. Ibid., 43–45 / GA39, 44–45.
22. Ibid., 65 / GA39, 71. See section 2.1 for my discussion of his earlier conflation of authenticity and essence.
23. Ibid., 108 / GA39, 119.
24. Ibid., 40 / GA39, 41.
25. Ibid., 58–59 / GA39, 63–64.
26. Ibid., 40 / GA39, 41. Cf. ibid., 4 /GA39, 5; 58 / GA39, 63; 64 / GA39, 70–71.
27. Ibid., 57 / GA39, 62.
28. Ibid., 60–61 / GA39, 66.
29. Ibid., 107 / GA39, 119.
30. Ibid., 108 / GA39, 119.
31. Ibid, 68 / GA39, 75.
32. Ibid., 198–99 / GA39, 217–18.
33. As quoted by Heidegger (ibid., 213 / GA39, 234).
34. Ibid, 214 / GA39, 235
35. Ibid., 216 / GA39, 237.
36. Ibid., 224 / GA39, 247.
37. Ibid., 243 / GA39, 268.

38. Ibid., 224 / GA39, 247.
39. Ibid., 226 / GA39, 250.
40. Ibid., 232 / GA39, 257.
41. Ibid., 185 / GA39, 203.
42. Ibid., 232 / GA39, 256.
43. Cf. ibid., 180–81 / GA39, 197–99; 185 / GA39, 203.
44. Ibid., 181–82 / GA39, 198–200.
45. Ibid., 183–84 / GA39, 201–02. Cf. ibid., 208–09 / GA39, 229.
46. Ibid., 183 / GA39, 201.
47. Cf. ibid., 31 / GA39, 32; 59 / GA39, 64;
48. Ibid., 184 / GA39, 202.
49. Ibid., 258 / GA39, 285.
50. Ibid., 184 / GA39, 202.
51. Ibid., 258 / GA39, 285. Cf. ibid., 261 / GA39, 287.
52. Ibid., 150 / GA39, 165.
53. Ibid., 132 / GA39, 150.
54. Ibid., 150 / GA39, 165.
55. Ibid., 149 / GA39, 164.
56. Ibid., 202 / GA39, 222.
57. Ibid., 199 / GA39, 218.

Chapter 4

Sigetics and the Silence of the Other Beginning in the Appropriating-Event

In his private manuscript from 1936 to 1938, *Contributions to Philosophy (Of the Event)*, Heidegger introduces his project as a thinking that attempts to cross toward the question concerning the truth as the "clearing-concealing" of beyng.[1] As a whole, truth involves beyng in its essential self-concealing and Da-sein as the "there" of the clearing of beyng and of the open realm in which beings come to stand in their manifestness. The thinking that transitions from the first beginning (with its metaphysics of objective presence) toward the other beginning of the thinking of beyng in its historicality belongs to and its appropriated by the event in which beyng itself essentially occurs. The course of the transitional thinking is one that traverses the realm of beyng in its concealedness to its clearing as appropriating-event.[2]

I maintain that as Heidegger outlines the course of thinking in the event of the truth of beyng, we discover the three different forms of silence in the event or the essential occurrence of beyng itself, as well as in the thinking that belongs to and is appropriated by it. Such thinking takes the form of a sigetic, and it consists in bearing silence (*Erschweigung*), which is the "prudent lawfulness of the silence-bearing activity" (*Erschweigens*).[3] However, while Heidegger speaks at length about the bearing silence that characterizes the appropriated thinking, he offers only a few hints on the forms of silence that pervade beyng itself in its clearing-concealing. I claim that in addition to the forms that human silence can take in the thinking of the event, the deeper forms pertain to the essence and the origin of language in relation to beyng in its truth, that is, to the primordial and primeval silences.

In Heidegger's rendition, thinking takes the form of a "thoughtful speaking" that is non-objectifying and instead belongs to beyng as its essential occurrence.[4] The disclosive character of this speaking resides in its being the "saying of beyng" that belongs to, is appropriated by, and names the event itself.[5] More specifically, it is the sonorous disclosure of beyng in its essential occurrence, which gathers and lets beyng resonate from its essence.[6] The possibilities of such sounding forth arise from the concealed essence of beyng, which is why "very little speaking 'of the event' is possible."[7] In other words, the truth of beyng itself, in its clearing-concealing, determines the limits to what can and cannot be said, by imposing silence. I maintain that thoughtful speaking would thereby be silenc*ed*.[8]

Heidegger continually characterizes the historicality of the event in which thoughtful speaking is granted its possibilities in terms of the abandonment by being in the age of machination and the gigantic. At issue is whether the human being will undergo an essential transformation from the metaphysical rational animal to Da-sein through the appropriating-event. The abandonment by being that marks the distortion of the essence of all that is includes the danger of beyng's refusal to appropriate the human being who is incapable of becoming Da-sein and is on the way to becoming the "*technologized animal*."[9] Thoughtful speaking would be silenced in and by this possible withholding of beyng as well. However, Heidegger asks whether another alternative to the withdrawal of beyng is possible as an appropriation in which humans experience the event with shock (*Erschrecken/Schrecken*), diffidence (*Scheu*), and restraint (*Verhaltenheit*) so as to propel themselves into Da-sein.[10] In my view, this question bespeaks a hope that he deposits in the transitional thinking at the same time that he spells out its fundamental attitudes or dispositions. Some of these dispositions will play key roles in the reticence and bearing silence that distinguish the thoughtful speaking, so they merit some consideration.

In its initial definition, restraint is the "proper 'will'" of shock, which involves an anticipatory readiness for the refusal of beyng and is turned toward its withdrawal. Heidegger identifies restraint as central to shock and diffidence.[11] Accordingly, restraint plays a key role in the silence and reticence of thoughtful speaking. Its centrality becomes increasingly evident as we probe into Heidegger's understanding of shock and diffidence.

Shock consists in being "taken aback" from what is familiar (which thereby becomes what is most unknown) and in being taken into the disclosive force of what conceals itself. As a fundamental disposition for the few, shock takes the specific form of being taken aback from the withdrawal of being from beings and taken into its disclosive self-concealment. I maintain that this form of being taken aback from and into could evidently involve different forms of silencing, for example, in the sense of being shocked into silence and in the sense of hearing and bearing silence as the truth of beyng unfolds.[12]

Heidegger describes diffidence as the "way of drawing near and remaining near to what is remote as such," and he claims that the necessity for reticence comes from diffidence. Such necessity ultimately arises here from the primeval need of beyng for those who seek after beyng, and preserve and shelter the truth of beyng.[13] They are the stewards or guardians of the "stillness of the passing by of the last god."[14] Heidegger claims that this stillness or "great" stillness itself "arises only out of keeping silent" and thus has its "origin" in restraint.[15] I maintain that stillness in this sense essentially pertains to Da-sein's disposition to be still, to endure, and to withstand the event; in a word, they mark the special moments of human silence in relation to the appropriating-event.[16] In this sense, Heidegger characterizes the "original seeking" of beyng in the manner of a questioning that bears silence as sheltering the "original finding" of beyng in its "self-concealing as such."[17]

Heidegger also assigns to stillness a key role in the decision (*Entscheidung*), which he emphasizes does not mean anything like making a choice. In his positive definition, he renders its meaning as de-cision (*Ent-scheidung*) that sunders and separates itself (*scheidet*) and thereby opens up as the clearing for the truth of beyng and the decision concerning the last god.[18] Heidegger places the decision in the "stillest stillness," and he depicts stillness as the site of the decision.[19] In the fundamental dispositions that determine their thoughtful speaking, the stewards forge forth the paths to the site of the stillness.[20] They are those who must find the "stillest and steepest paths" that lead out of the forgottenness of beyng to ground the site where beyng essentially occurs.[21] As the future ones, the stewards of stillness are those whose anticipatory resoluteness is attuned to the truth of beyng. This attunement is reflected in their being the still and the hidden ones who hear and preserve what is most hidden.[22] The few who hear in the projective, futural manner are those who project the truth of beyng, its unconcealedness into beings, and in this manner project from the "stillness out of which beyng (as event) becomes perceptible."[23] In this role, they forge ahead to prepare the human being for hearing the truth of beyng. At issue in this preparatory role is whether the "future ones have an ear for the sound of the resonating," in which the abandonment by being is experienced, and which "must be made to sound forth" to prepare for the other beginning.[24] As those who think forward in the transition to the other beginning of the truth of being in its historicality, they are the creative ones whose inventive thinking and thoughtful speaking projects to the moment when we would be able to hear and to name beyng adequately.[25]

I maintain that stillness as a fundamental disposition that involves the ability to hear beyng would evidently involve the ability to be silent as well. Being still is not only associated with the keeping silent from which it arises but also with the reticence that defines the "[n]earness to the last god."[26] The pinnacle of being still is thus exemplified in the thinking, where "there remains only the simplest saying of the plainest image in purest reticence."[27] Once again, the central role of restraint comes to the fore, now as "openness for the reticent nearness of the essential occurrence of beyng."[28]

I claim that the fundamental attitudes discussed above (restraint, shock, and diffidence) can be extrapolated from Heidegger's characterization of thoughtful speaking as a "*directive*" to "the few," which calls not only for awareness of the "danger of the refusal" of beyng but also for being prepared for its "overcoming."[29] In their awareness and preparedness, the few and rare follow the "hidden" path of "solitude" in the inceptual thinking of the other beginning.[30] This is the path of "concealment" and of "byways" in philosophy, which must retreat and become inaccessible to "the many."[31] The many are obviously those who hear and respond only to "the gigantic and the loud."[32] Thus, in the path that is inaccessible for the many, the thinkers "shelter" the truth of beyng through the "ponderous slowness" of their questioning and as they "inconspicuously" take their "ever-hesitant step[s]." The path of concealment here is also that of the poet, who "veils the truth in images." Such paths are determined by the sigetic principle whereby reticence concerning the truth of beyng becomes "more unavoidable" as thoughtful speaking about beyng becomes "more necessary."[33]

I maintain that thoughtful speaking requires the fundamental disposition of restraint with regard to the *constraints* that are determined in language by beyng in its self-concealing, withdrawal, and possible refusal. In this regard, silence is imposed upon the few and rare—they are silenced by the self-concealing of beyng as words "fail" them. However, I claim that such self-concealing is also a clearing that opens up the possibility of an inceptual revelation of beyng in language—in words that show and in names that point to the truth of beyng.[34] Restraint thus enables the few to withstand the abyssal-ground of the clearing-concealing as they bear silence and remain reticent.[35]

Still, thoughtful speaking must speak, if it is to disclose the event. Moreover, it is itself appropriated to be the saying of the event. As Heidegger puts it later, in *The History of Beyng* (1938–40), "Thinking is 'of' beyng, and thus attuned opens, in its saying, the truth of beyng as sustainment into the simplicity of the word that keeps silent."[36] He thus insists in the *Contributions to Philosophy (Of the Event)* that we have to understand that "the clearing brings *what is self-concealing* into the open."[37] In this sense, the task for thoughtful speaking is "to bring the essential occurrence of beyng to the word."[38] My contention is that as the speaking of the transitional thinking, it crosses from one abyssal silence toward another. The language of the first beginning has declined into the everyday language, which has itself degenerated into idle chatter. It is the metaphysical language of beings, in which the truth of beyng "cannot be said."[39] I claim that this limit to saying is the first abyssal silence, where words fail and do not yet come to speech. The other abyssal silence lies in the realms that are "still closed to us because we do not know the truth of beyng," and these would be the concealed realms of the language of beyng. Perhaps the truth of beyng could be said in this language, but Heidegger maintains that saying has to let the capacity to hear emerge with it.[40] In my interpretation, he thereby suggests that the capacity for hearing the truth of beyng is lacking, that in the loud age of machination and gigantism we are deaf to the abyssal silence of beyng.[41]

Facing the two abyssal silences and the impossibility of inventing a new language for beyng, transitional thinking can still be an inventive thinking (*Er-denken*) of beyng. Thus, its speaking can arise from "a sort of transformed saying," which says and thereby shows the language of beings *as* the language of beyng.[42] In the same vein, Heidegger characterizes inceptual thinking as "letting beyng protrude into beings out of the silence-bearing utterance of the grasping word."[43] The language of beyng still remains unsaid, but it is intimated in the silent showing through the *as*-structure. At the same time, Heidegger views this saying as a "transformation" of language that "presses us into" the closed realms of the truth of beyng.[44] The thoughtful speaking aims to be transformative as well in this sense.

Heidegger attaches great importance to the transformative power of the thoughtful speaking that silently says the language of beyng as it speaks the language of beings; ultimately, it involves the human being's transformation.[45] In my reading, he envisions this transformation from the rational animal to Da-sein as a possibility that can arise as the silent saying effects a turning around of the meaning (*Bedeutungsumschlag*) of words. The meaning of a word in the ordinary language of the first beginning discloses what is familiar to us—namely, beings—and in this manner conceals beyng.[46] Heidegger thus outlines the method of turning around the meanings of the words as part of the directive for thoughtful speaking toward transforming thinking, though it is "under the power of the same word."[47] It bears noting that the saying of beyng, which must be a naming of the event and of the "between," is based on the decision that "*always interprets between* [zwischendeutig]" and is thus unavoidably ambiguous.[48]

The stratagem of the inversion of thinking belongs to the inceptual thinking that is reticent insofar as it is sigetic, which means that the silence-bearing activity of transitional thinking is essentially related to the truth of beyng.[49] A fundamental principle of sigetics, which is higher than any of the laws in metaphysical logic, is that saying can only speak "*out of* the truth of beyng" and thus cannot go toward and say beyng "immediately."[50] Therefore, the bearing of silence is based on the fundamental disposition of restraint in awaiting, in anticipatory readiness, for what is first—the clearing-concealing of beyng.[51] Restraint is also key to forestalling the forgottenness of beyng. The few must thus constantly remind themselves that, as humans, they too must be exposed to beings while beyng conceals itself.[52] In their mindful awareness of beyng's essential occurrence as self-concealment, the inceptual thinkers in the transition toward the other beginning of the truth of beyng differ even from the inceptual thinkers of the first beginning. The first thinkers' fundamental word for truth—*a-lētheia*—"means un-concealment and the un-concealed itself," and they thereby experience concealment only as "what is to be removed (α-)."[53] In Heidegger's rendition, this means that their inquiry into *alētheia* does not take into account the concealing itself and its own clearing, but instead focuses on what is unconcealed.[54] Still, with this inaugural word of the first beginning, the concealing is not simply annulled, but instead first emerges to be grasped in its essence.[55] This is the legacy for the thinkers of the other beginning as the stewards of the "stillest stillness" in which the decision that arises has the "longest history."[56]

I claim that Heidegger is hinting at the primeval silence when he characterizes sigetics in terms of its search for the "*truth of the essential occurrence* of beyng," and he identifies this truth as the "intimating-resonating concealment (the mystery) of the event (the hesitant withholding)."[57] The primeval silence pervades the originary self-concealment of beyng as well as its self-concealing withdrawal. This deepest of silences also pervades the soundless intimating-resonating through which beyng unconceals itself to appropriate those who can hear and sound forth its truth. Such is the mystery: the self-concealing of beyng in its essential occurrence, in the supreme silence of the appropriating-event.[58]

As the stewards of stillness, the few and rare are those who are able to bear silence and hear the silent call of beyng. The call to the leap into appropriation, which Heidegger identifies as the "great stillness of the most concealed self-knowledge," concerns the leap of Da-sein to itself as belonging to the event.[59] In this self-knowledge, the human being becomes the "there" of the clearing-concealing of beyng, which is the most concealed possibility of the event. The great stillness that characterizes this self-knowledge is the human being's disposition to withstand the event of the clearing-concealing of beyng. Put otherwise, the great stillness involves enduring the open realm of concealment and withstanding the openness of the self-concealing of beyng. To be the "there" is thus to stand out in the open realm of beyng in which beings are manifest.[60]

Significantly, Heidegger claims that "[e]very language of Da-sein originates" in the great stillness and is "thus in essence silence."[61] My contention is that in referring to the languages of Da-sein, this statement pertains to language in its historicality, which is itself determined in and by the truth of beyng. All historical languages thus have their origin in the clearing-concealing of beyng and, in this sense, have their essential source in the primeval silence of its truth. However, it is important to note that Heidegger is addressing here the question concerning the origination of these languages in Da-sein and is thus focusing on its being, on what is distinctive in Da-sein as the "there" of the truth of beyng. This is the truth of Da-sein, that is, what Heidegger had earlier called "disclosedness," and now calls the "openness of self-concealing, begun by the *understanding of being*."[62]

My claim is that the silence in question pertains to the human being. In this light, we can see that the stillness or the great stillness of Da-sein in its self-knowledge is the "there" where all languages originate. Every language is in essence silence in this specific regard, that is, in relation to Da-sein's being. Language as the human ability to speak is to say in word-sounds and, in this saying, it discloses, shows and names something as something. This essential ability is rooted in Da-sein's openness to beyng in its clearing-concealing, which is what enables Da-sein to grasp what is cleared—beings in their being—and what is concealed and self-concealing—beyng in its unconcealing. The necessary condition for showing something as something in sonorous speech, in a language, is this grasping in the open realm. Every language thus has its essence in the silence of the "there." However, Da-sein's silence is evidently not a sufficient condition. I claim that we have to consider the relation between language as such and beyng to probe for deeper—primordial and primeval—silences that pervade the clearing-concealing of beyng.

Heidegger takes pains to distinguish his reflections on language from the metaphysics of language that is based on the concept of *logos*, which is understood in terms of assertion, representation, and reason. The metaphysical definitions of language as the tool, possession, or work of the human being draw back to the definition of the human being as the rational animal. Heidegger argues that the same metaphysical determinations that are at play in the concept of the rational animal (body, soul, spirit) operate in the concept of language (with body as the word, soul as the mood, and spirit as what is thought and represented). The view of language as a symbol of the human essence is the culmination of this "anthropological" view of language. Heidegger's assessment of the symbolic concept of language in this context is unusually positive; it "touches" on what is "proper to language: the *sound* and phonetic structure of the word, the tone and meaning of the word." However, he remains critical of its metaphysical connotations, even when "word" is understood in terms of "uttering and keeping silent" with regard to what is said and not said. Given his own idea of historical languages in terms of sonorous saying, hearing, and bearing silence, I believe that it makes sense that he would want to point beyond the metaphysical distinction and suggest how it can be overcome. This is precisely the approach that he takes here by insisting that we must first ask how does language relate to beyng, and this entails asking the proto-linguistic question, "How does the essence of language originate in the essential occurrence of beyng."[63]

At the same time, Heidegger spells out what could be identified as the hermeneutical presuppositions of this question. In this vein, he declares that the human being and language "both *belong* equiprimordially to beyng."[64] He also asserts that it opens up an alternative to the metaphysical view that relates language to humans and beings. In fact, he explicitly justifies his approach here via such presuppositions as an authentic essential question in which there is no other way to determine the essence of language than by naming its origin.[65] Yet, I would like draw attention to the fact that he does not expressly answer *how* language originates out of beyng. Neither does he actually say *what* is the origin of language. He only says *where/when* it is found, namely, in the essential occurrence of beyng. At the same time, he does hint the answers, and these point to the truth and the silence of beyng itself.

Heidegger claims that sigetics is where we can first grasp language in its essence. This proposal evidently points to silence. However, I maintain that, in its fundamental sense, this is not the silence that belongs to Da-sein, the human silence, but the primeval silence, the silence that belongs to beyng itself. Heidegger thus asserts that Da-sein's essential possibility of bearing silence "arises out of the essentially occurring origin of language itself."[66] This essentially occurring origin of language is the truth of beyng, which as he emphatically declares "*is the beyng of truth,*" that is, the clearing-concealing in which beyng conceals itself.[67] As I have argued before, the concealing aspect of truth takes the form of silence; beyng conceals itself in its silence. It follows that the clue to how language originates out of beyng lies in the primeval silence in which beyng conceals itself and from which it *un*conceals itself in the clearing-concealing. This inference seems to fit with one of items Heidegger lists at the start of his comments on beyng and the origin of language, which he identifies as "the echo" belonging to the event.[68] I maintain that language is thereby the reverberation of the silent essential occurrence of beyng in its truth, in its clearing-concealing. Put otherwise: language in its silent essence is the echo of the primeval silence.

Heidegger also takes a more direct route to the origin of language in the final section (281) of his *Contributions*.[69] Here, he reformulates the trope of the echo in terms of the call and the fourfold, where the gods call the earth, and in this call a world echoes and resonates as Da-sein. These are the conditions for the *historical existence* of language. So, silence pervades the call, the sounding forth of the earth, and the resounding of the world. The call's resonating as Da-sein implies that language *in its essence*, as the word, is silent as well. This suggests the primordial silence. It is in the event of the call that language becomes the speaking in word-sounds, the sonorous speech of the human being through which the word grounds history. Silence plays an important role in what Heidegger describes as the problem of meditating on *the* language that is also *our* language, that is, language in its historical existence, which has its origin in and belongs to beyng. The immanence of the question concerning the essence of language is inescapable. In this vein, Heidegger characterizes his own meditation here as "falling into the abyss" of the relation between language and beyng, so that we find "no answer" to the question.[70] Thus, I claim that it is the primeval silence of beyng that pervades through the questioning, and its answer is silent in the supreme sense.

In the final words of the *Contributions*, Heidegger identifies silence as the "ground" of language. I claim that this is the primeval silence of beyng in its truth, for he also refers to language here as "*spoken or silent*." The latter possibilities of speaking and being silent are those that pertain to Da-sein. Thus, Heidegger portrays this language in which the human being is able to speak or be silent at the crossroads between the "grounding" of Da-sein that humanizes beings and our dehumanization as a living present-at-hand thing and consequently that of beings. I claim that the silence that belongs to beyng is what Heidegger depicts here as the "most concealed holding to the measure."[71] Its supreme concealedness is that of beyng in its self-concealing. In my interpretation, measure as such pertains to what he calls the "temporal-spatial playing field of the truth of beyng."[72] The playing field is also that of the "there" and it is thereby the playing field within which Da-sein itself is grounded.[73] In its clearing-concealing, truth unfolds as the temporal-spatial playing field in which beyng essentially occurs and the human being is appropriated as its "there."

Heidegger explains that language "*holds* to the measure, in the sense that it first posits the measure" and that it is the positing or setting of the measure "as the originating essential occurrence of what is fitting and of its joining (event)."[74] My sense is that this explanation points to silence as the concealed holding to the measure, which language holds to by setting. Such setting involves the gathering of what is unconcealed and what is concealed in the open realm of truth as the clearing-concealing. In this sense, language in its essence, as the word, is the structuring or articulation of the playing field of beyng. This is the pre-linguistic role of the word. Its structuring is what enables the human being to speak in word-sounds, to say and thus to show, to name and thus to point to what is concealed and unconcealed. It is in this sense that Heidegger calls for the meditation on the essence of language as the "naming that founds the truth of beyng."[75] It is also in this sense that he looks forward to the other beginning in which beings "become nameable in language and belong to the reticence" of beyng in its withdrawal from the calculation of beings, at the same time that it "squanders its essence" for the fourfold.[76]

The few and rare who are themselves reticent in their thoughtful speaking are those who go down to the abyssal ground of beyng.[77] Thus, their saying as the "saying that bears silence" is "what grounds," and bearing silence itself is only possible insofar as it "arises out of the essentially occurring origin of language itself," that is, out of the primeval silence of beyng.[78] In this sense, the restraint of the inceptual thinkers is attuned to this deepest of silences insofar as it is "subservient to the gentle measure—enduring it through silence."[79]

In conclusion, Heidegger's sigetic reflections on the appropriating-event take more decisive steps in the development of the concept of silence in its primordial and primeval forms as he traces more direct links between the essence and the origin of language and the truth of beyng. At the same time, his idea of the human form of silence takes on, not only many more defined characteristics as the thoughtful speaking of transitional thinking but also a more intimate relation to the deeper silences. Figure 4.1 summarizes the forms that silence takes in Heidegger's thinking of *Ereignis* at this stage:

(A) Human silence (transitional thinking and thoughtful speaking in sigetics)

- Reticence (restraint, shock, diffidence)
    - Bearing silence
    - Stillness (in disposition, decision, projection, stewardship)
    - Path of concealment of the few and the rare that is inaccessible to the many
    - Intimating the language of beyng (through the as-structure)
- Being silenced

________ (1) Linguistic level ________

(B) Primordial silence of (the essence of) language

- Abyssal silence in the language of beings
- Abyssal silence of the language of beyng
- Echo of the primeval silence

________ (2) Pre-linguistic level ________

(C) Primeval silence of the event of the truth (clearing-concealing) of beyng

- Origin of language in its essence
- Call of beyng
- Mystery of beyng

________ (3) Proto-linguistic level ________

Figure 4.1

In the next chapter, I show how Heidegger applies his sigetic principles in his confrontation with Herder on the question concerning the origin of language.

NOTES

1. Martin Heidegger, *Contributions to Philosophy (Of the Event)*, trans. Richard Rojcewicz and Daniela Vallega-Neu (Bloomington and Indianapolis: Indiana University Press, 2012), 87 / GA65, 70; 94–95 / GA65, 75–76; sections 224–26.
2. Ibid., 25 / GA65, 3.
3. Ibid., 94 / GA65, 78.
4. Ibid., 26 / GA65, 4.
5. Ibid., 99 / GA65, 83. Cf. ibid., 467 / GA65, 484.
6. Ibid., 26 / GA65, 4.
7. Ibid., 29 / GA65, 7.
8. In a later rendering (1941–42), Heidegger says as much with regard to speechlessness: "Indeed it happens to us occasionally that we are 'speechless' in amazement, joy, horror, bliss. But we have no inking of speechlessness itself in its event-related essence. What appears to be the absence of speech, i.e., the absence of vocables and words, is, thought inceptually and essentially, only the pure event of the word as the disposing voice of beyng." Heidegger, *The Event*, trans. Richard Rojcewicz (Bloomington and Indianapolis: Indiana University Press, 2013), 146 / GA71, 171–72.
9. Cf. Heidegger, *Contributions to Philosophy (Of the Event)*, 25 / GA65, 3; 29 / GA65 7–8; 44 / GA65, 23; 113 / GA65, 98; 128 / GA65, 116; 241 / GA65, 238; 395 / GA65, 406; 426 / GA65, 442; 477 / GA65, 495.
10. Ibid., 29 / GA65, 8.
11. Ibid.
12. Ibid., 36 / GA65, 15.
13. Ibid.
14. Ibid., 38 / GA65, 17.
15. Ibid., 54–55 / GA65, 35–36. See also, ibid., section 6; 111 / GA65, 96.
16. Cf. ibid., 38 / GA 65, 17; 54 / GA65, 34–35; 130 / GA65, 118; 133 / GA65, 121.
17. Ibid., 96 / GA65, 80.
18. Ibid., 103 / GA65, 88.
19. Cf. ibid., 112 / GA65, 97; 115 / GA65, 100; 254 / GA65, 252.
20. Ibid., 402 / GA65, 414. Cf. Heidegger, *The History of Beyng*, trans. William McNeill and Jeffrey Powell (Bloomington, Indiana: Indiana University Press, 2015), 119 / GA69, 138–39.
21. Ibid., 242 / GA65, 238–39.
22. Ibid., 387 / GA65, 395. Cf. ibid., 306 / GA65, 309.
23. Ibid., 44 / GA65, 23.
24. Ibid., 124 / GA65, 112. Cf. ibid., 26 / GA65, 5–6.
25. Ibid., 446 / GA65, 463. Cf. ibid., 408 / GA65, 422.

26. Ibid., 33 / GA65, 12.

27. Ibid., 88 / GA65, 72.

28. Ibid., 55 / GA65, 72. Daniela Vallega-Neu focuses on similar points in her characterization of Heidegger's own reticence and silence in the *Contributions* in terms of a "language of resistance" that is bound to restraint and based on the grounding mood of diffidence. See: Daniela Vallega-Neu, "Heidegger's Reticence: From *Contributions* to Das *Ereignis* and toward *Gelassenheit*" in *Research in Phenomenology* 45(2015): 1–32, especially 12–14.

29. Ibid., 30 / GA65, 8.

30. See, for example, ibid., 33–34 / GA65, 12–13; 66 / GA65, 47; 122–23 / GA65, 110; 397–98 / GA65, 414; 418 / GA65, 434; 454 / GA65, 471. For a critique of this requisite, see: Francisco Gonzalez, "And the Rest is *Sigetik*: Silencing Logic and Dialectic in Heidegger's *Beiträge zur Philosophie*" in *Research in Phenomenology* 38(2008): 358–91. Gonzalez claims that sigetics is thus "opposed to dialogue" and is ultimately "*a dictatorship of silence*" (386–87). My sense is that he mistakenly equates solitude with the impossibility of a dialogue between those who are solitary.

31. Ibid., 38 / GA65, 17.

32. Ibid., 112 / GA65, 97. See also, ibid., 53 / GA65, 34; 109 / GA65, 94–95.

33. Ibid., 40 / GA65, 19.

34. Ibid., 55–56 / GA65, 36.

35. Heidegger explicitly connects the abyssal-ground with truth (ibid., 371 / GA65, 380).

36. Heidegger, *The History of Beyng*, 99 / GA69, 117–18.

37. Heidegger, *Contributions to Philosophy (Of the Event),* 350 / GA65, 257.

38. Ibid., 244 / GA65, 241.

39. Ibid., 94 / GA65, 78.

40. Ibid. Cf. ibid., 33 / GA65, 12; 89 / GA65, 73; 446 / GA65, 463.

41. Heidegger's private notes from 1939 to 1941 show continuity in the contrast between the age of the loud or noisy machination and the other beginning of the silence of beyng. For some examples, see: Heidegger, *Ponderings XII–XV: Black Notebooks* 1939–1941, trans. Richard Rojcewicz (Bloomington and Indianapolis: Indiana University Press, 2017), 42 / GA94 XII–XV, 54; 63 / GA94 XII–XV, 79–80; 73 / GA94 XII–XV, 92.

42. Heidegger, *Contributions to Philosophy (Of the Event)*, 94 / GA65, 78.

43. Ibid., 76 / GA65, 58.

44. Ibid., 94 / GA65, 78.

45. Ibid., 100 / GA65, 83–84.

46. Ibid., 99 / GA65, 83.

47. Ibid.

48. Ibid., 467 / GA65, 484. Cf. ibid., 85 / GA65, 68; 419 / GA65, 435; 439 / GA65, 455; 446 / GA65, 463.

49. Ibid., 76 / GA65, 58.

50. Ibid., 94–95 / GA65, 78–79.

51. Ibid., 342 / GA65, 348.

52. Ibid., 256–57 / GA65, 255.

53. Ibid., 344 / GA65, 350.
54. Ibid. Cf. ibid., 333 / GA65, 355.
55. Ibid.
56. Ibid., 114 / GA65, 100.
57. Ibid., 95 / GA65, 78.
58. Heidegger also alludes to the mysterious call of beyng in its supreme silence when he discusses the turning of the event and the plight of the abandonment of beyng (ibid., 395–97 / GA65, 407–08).
59. Ibid., 396 / GA65, 408.
60. Cf. ibid., 222 / GA65, 217; 257 / GA65 255; 288 / GA65, 289; 298–99 / GA65, 301; 300 / GA65, 303; 315 / GA65, 318.
61. Ibid., 396 / GA65, 408.
62. Ibid., 292 / GA65, 294–95.
63. Ibid., 480–84 / GA65, 500–03.
64. Ibid., 479 / GA65, 497.
65. Ibid., 480–82 / GA65, 499–500.
66. Ibid., 95 / GA65, 79.
67. Ibid., 110 / GA65, 95. Cf. ibid., 260 / GA65, 258.
68. Ibid., 478–79 / GA65, 497.
69. Ibid., 490–91 / GA65, 510.
70. Ibid., 483 / GA65, 501.
71. Ibid., 491 / GA65, 510.
72. Ibid., 26 / GA65, 5.
73. See, for example, ibid., 42 / GA65, 22; 103 / GA65, 87; 232 / GA65, 127.
74. Ibid., 491 / GA65, 510.
75. Ibid., 183–84 / GA65, 177.
76. Ibid., 469 / GA65, 486.
77. See, for example, ibid., 29 / GA65, 7; 83 / GA65, 66; 388 / GA65, 397.
78. Ibid., 96 / GA65, 79.
79. Ibid., 86 / GA65, 69.

Chapter 5

The Silent Origin of Language in the Confrontation with Herder

The final section of Heidegger's *Contributions to Philosophy (Of the Event)*, titled "Language (its Origin)," anticipates the task that he undertakes in the summer of 1939 with his graduate seminar, *On the Essence of Language. The Metaphysics of Language and the Essencing of the Word. Concerning Herder's Treatise* On the Origin of Language. Herder's essay serves as a passageway for Heidegger's thinking in the crossing, which appears in outlines and fragments throughout this work. In Heidegger's initial definition here, the path of the crossing starts from the metaphysics of language toward the leap into the being-historical thinking of the word as the original essence of language and as the essencing of the truth of beyng.[1] His interpretation of Herder in this light takes the form of a confrontation that sets apart (*Aus-einander-setzung*), through which he repeatedly launches a multifront critique of the metaphysical presuppositions in Herder's theory. At the same time, he issues positive, though heavily qualified, assessments of Herder's "sensing" of deeper meanings that align with the crossing.[2]

I maintain that what Heidegger interprets as Herder's intuitive insights into hearing operates as a springboard for the development of his own reflections on hearkening and on silence in its relation to the word and the truth of beyng. The poetry of Stephan George, which Heidegger interprets as a crossing word in its "intimation" of the word of beyng, also serves as channel for his own thoughts on silence in terms of the refusal of beyng.[3] In what follows, I will first focus on Heidegger's overall critique of the metaphysics of language and then turn to the intimations of silence that he appropriates in his interpretations of Herder and George.

One of Heidegger's main contentions is that the question of the origin of language that Herder proposes to answer is itself metaphysical insofar as it asks for the ground of an extant or present-at-hand entity, defines "essence" in terms of beingness, and understands "origin" as origination, causation, and condition of possibility.[4] In this light, Heidegger not only situates Herder within traditional metaphysics and in the philosophy of language that emerges in the Enlightenment but also equates him with Hamman, Sußmilch, and Humboldt, and traces his influence in Grimm and the subsequent metaphysics of language.[5]

In Heidegger's critical rendition, Herder's argument that the human being invents language by virtue of its distinctive capacity of reflective awareness (*Besonnenheit*) is imbued in metaphysics. Herder's idea of language as a human distinction betrays the definition of the human being as the rational animal—the metaphysical *zōon logon ekhon*.[6] Furthermore, his view of language in terms of *ratio et oratio* (reason and speech) is based on the metaphysical interpretation of *logos*.[7] Uncovering the metaphysical *ratio*, Heidegger critically points to Herder's commonality with Hamman, Humboldt, and Hegel in the conception of language in terms of reason.[8] Herder's central concept of reflective awareness is metaphysical as well, for it is tantamount to the representation of objects by reason.[9] Heidegger also argues that, in spite of Herder's influence in German Romanticism, through his "critique of 'rationalism' and 'sensualism'" and his "*turning away from 'logic,'*" Herder "remains stuck in the *logos* of reason."[10] The metaphysical *oratio*, in turn, underlies Herder's conception of language as communication that informs about objects, making them noticeable by making them manifest to others.[11] Moreover, his view of language in terms of sonorous signification and expression is based on the metaphysical definition of *logos* in terms of the *phōnē semantikē* and *phōnē meta phantasias*.[12]

Heidegger repeatedly casts in a critical light Herder's thesis that the origin of language lies in the formation of inner and outer marks by reflective awareness.[13] In Heidegger's portrayal, this thesis is steeped in the metaphysics of reason and representation: "Use-of-reason is *mark-formation* insofar as through it ob-ject is brought to stand and to self-subsistence and kept freely available."[14] This view involves the metaphysical reduction where "reason is language from inside. . . . Language is reason from outside."[15] Word-formation is mark-formation in that a word is a "mark of a distinct reflection." The word is thereby reduced to a "mark-sign" that is "*furnished with sounds,*" and language itself is reduced to a "*sign*ifying, letting-notice" and a "sign-production." Heidegger accordingly highlights here the "traditional metaphysical appearance of language" in terms of beingness, representation, and objectification in Herder's account of the origin of language.[16]

Heidegger argues that Herder's claim that the human being has language "already as an animal" and his claim that humans "distinguish themselves precisely through language from all animals" are compatible insofar as they are based on the same metaphysical presuppositions concerning language and the rational animal. The implications that Heidegger draws from Herder's first claim—that the human being is an "animal" and that there is "an animal language (sounding in sensations)"— are constantly repeated throughout the course and thus appear to be as problematic as the implications of the second claim—that language "*distinguishes*" the human being and that the human being is not "*only*" animal.[17]

Heidegger also takes great pains to reveal the metaphysics in the analogy and distinction in kind that Herder develops between the human being and the animal.[18] More fundamentally, he emphasizes that Herder fails to establish the "decisive *essential* difference" between human (in its "*openness*" to being) and animal (captivated and dazed in its wrap).[19] He also fails to take the "essential steps" of bringing the human being to its "essential ground—which is the abysmal-ground of being [*Ab-grund des Seyns*]!"[20] Moreover, because Herder begins with the *animalitas* of the *animal rationale,* he is never able to get beyond the animalistic determination of the human being.[21] Heidegger also suggests that Herder's general characterization of language in terms of the sounding of sensations fails to establish the essential difference between human and animal in terms of reflective awareness and its formation of inner marks. Herder even fails in establishing the *rationalitas* of the human animal and its language.[22]

Heidegger views the problem of circularity in Herder's argument—that is, the reciprocal definition of human being and language—as a product of metaphysical thinking as well.[23] His coinage of the term "inventing-by-finding" (*Er-findung*) to characterize Herder's idea of language as an invention (*Erfindung*) of the human being highlights this circularity.[24] Finally, he also underscores the metaphysical underpinnings in the idea of invention as the production of something present-at-hand.[25]

By way of contrast with Herder's metaphysics of language, Heidegger defines his own approach as a "reflection on the 'origin' (ground of the essence) of language from the word; the word, however, as essencing of the truth of beyng."[26] I claim that such essencing is the appropriating-event of the unconcealedness of beyng, though he does not explicitly define truth in these terms here. Heidegger specifically distinguishes his project from the metaphysical question: "The essence of language—*not* asked metaphysically: 'Essence' . . . rather *belongingness in being* [das Seyn] . . . *in the event as deliverance.*"[27] My contention is that, though he does not define "deliverance" (*Austrag*) here either, it suggests the *un*concealedness in which beyng wrests itself free from concealedness and lets the essence of freedom emerge as such.[28]

In the crossing toward being-historical thinking, the metaphysical claim, "The human being has language," comes into question with the dictum, "The word has the human being."[29] Heidegger stresses that the crossing is not a reversal, but an essential transformation, which is not a matter of deposing metaphysics, but of "[b]reaking through" the metaphysical circle in the reciprocal definition of language and the human being with the dictum "language as word."[30] He also suggests that his reflection thereby probes deeper than metaphysics: "Where the *proper* origin of the *deeper essence* of language—as saga and saying? In being [*Seyn*]. The word 'of' being [*'des' Seyns*]."[31]

Heidegger applies the (transformative, rupturing, and probing) principles of the crossing in his assessment of Herder's notion of the sense of hearing as the middle of the thinking *sensorium commune*. In Herder's characterization of the human being as a "hearkening, attentive creature," whose reflective awareness of its sensations enables it to mark, collect, and recollect them, the sense of hearing is the middle of all senses in various respects, with feeling or touching as one extreme and seeing as the other. Hearing is the most apt sense for language, understood in terms of sonorous reception (inner marks) and sonorous expression (outer marks, for example, words, interjections). As the middle, it is the unifying and mediating sense for all the other senses. Herder thus calls the ear "the first teacher of language" and claims that we become "hearing through all our senses."[32]

Heidegger's crossing interpretation also works to show "what is *un*said" in Herder's "*metaphysical*" reflection on the origin of language.[33] In his critical appropriation of Herder's metaphysical concept of hearing and hearkening, Heidegger juxtaposes the being-historical meaning of the hearkening (*Horchen*) that obeys-by-hearing (*gehor-sam*) and belongs (*gehören*) to the truth of beyng.[34] I claim that hearkening in the latter sense takes form in the human being's silence; as Heidegger suggests in a question, in "the silencing of the *silence* of the 'there' of *being-there?*"[35] My sense is that the human being's silence here is the silencing (*Erschweigen*), while the silence or stillness (*die Stille*) of the "there" of being-there is the primeval silence of beyng. Heidegger also asserts that the "freedom" of the "there" in hearkening "in itself as *belongingness* in the appropriating-event—the *silence* of being [*des Seyns*] itself, is *word*."[36] So, the silencing of being-there in its hearkening to the word as the primordial silence is a crossing that *breaks through* Herder's hearkening, attentive creature.

Herder's metaphysical notion of the reflective awareness that invents language by first forming inner words undergoes what Heidegger would count as an "*essential* transformation," with the deeper meaning of the hearkening to the word in relation to the silence of beyng and the silencing of being-there. However, in Herder, the inner language is non-sonorous and the external language is sonorous, but the distinction is based on the metaphysical "'acoustical'-'phonetical'" concept of sound.[37] Moreover, he seems to (mis-)understand silence as the "ab-sence of noises?" instead of the "more essential" silence.[38] Herder also confusedly assigns to hearing the primacy over hearkening, without seeing that "hearing" is "not from ear and tone, not from sense of hearing—but from *hearkening and obeying*."[39] More to the point, he is metaphysically blind, even with regard to his own concepts.[40] Thus, in Heidegger's probing assessment, Herder does not get to the deeper sense of hearing, which is the hearkening that pertains to Da-sein's silencing, in "the *insistence that hearkens and awaits in the clearing*."[41] The word is that "*original clearing*"; it is the "event" of the opening of beyng in its *un*concealedness. The word is silent in a primordial sense, as the "[*s*]*ilencing of the deliverance*," which means that it harbors (silently disclosing) beyng it is un*concealedness*. I claim that this is what Heidegger suggests here when he says that the word "*preserves discretely the clearing of the there*."[42] So, it goes without saying that Herder also misses the deeper connection between hearkening and the original silent essence of language.

From Heidegger's crossing perspective, Herder's metaphysical hearkening is ultimately "the deeper essence of reason," the "removed gathering (*logos*)."[43] So, Herder fails to recognize that the meaning of hearkening is "being-attentive-on" (*auf-merken*) and this means the "understanding of being."[44] In his forgetting of being, Herder also seems to confuse the direction of attention (*Merken*) and hearkening: "Herder appears to assign attention to the inner word and its 'genesis' and 'hearkening' to the outer and its genesis as the essential conditions! But: attention goes outwards ('beings') and hearkening goes 'inwards' (being)."[45]

Heidegger's assessment of Herder's idea of hearing as "the middle" of the senses is perhaps somewhat more positive, though it highlights Herder's unwittingness: "What Herder *senses* with the 'middle' character of 'hearing' is the in-between and in the midst of the *clearing*."[46] Though Herder's intuition regarding hearing, where "ear and tone themselves essence in the 'in-between' . . . *indicates* the deeper sense of *perception*," he remains within metaphysics. For Heidegger, Herder's metaphysical limits pertain not only to the *rationalitas* that defines the middle of the senses but also to the *animalitas* of the sense of hearing that allows for an "*animal 'hearing'* (scent, tension, 'to prick up the ears')," in an *animal* language, with its sounding of sensations.[47]

I claim that Heidegger's critical reflections on Herder also give us a glimpse into the development of his own concepts of sound and sounding as he questions the metaphysical definition of human language as "the *expressed, sounding reason*" and of language in general as "*sounding in sensations.*"[48] In Herder, sounding is the verbal expression that takes place in the outer mark, particularly in what Heidegger calls "the word-sound that sounds," which Herder understands in the metaphysical (acoustic or phonetical) sense.[49] However, what I identify as a pre-linguistic probing shows that the deeper essence of language as saying is "not 'expression,' making noticeable," but, as he suggests, to disclose. Saying "indeed" involves "'sounding,' but this having the character of strife (earth—world), a grounding *of a project, of a foundation.*"[50] The deeper sense of "sounding," then, is "grounded in the essence of being [*des Seyns*] itself" and, as "happening of the strife of earth *and* world," it "presupposes already the strife and the clearing."[51]

Going even deeper, toward what I call the proto-linguistic level, Heidegger claims that both the strife and the clearing have an essential relationship with silence, insofar as sounding is "not essentially related to the tone and sound, but *to the openness and clearing* of being and, that is, to the silence and the rending of the silence in the strife of world and earth."[52] Though Heidegger poses the following question concerning the relation between silence and sound, his answer is already contained in the question: "*Sound* ('perceptual')—and '*silence.*' *Silence* only privation—or ground of the 'sound'? or even abysmal-ground?"[53] In a more conclusive formulation, he says, "The sound—not first relative to ear, but to *silence*—that is, not 'relative,' but a manner of silence itself. Its rending—the 'rift.'"[54] The same applies in the following question/answer about sounding in relation to silence: "Or does *sounding* belong in a *different more essential* reality, and which is this which grounds and first gives 'space' for the sound? The clearing of being [*des Seyns*]."[55] I maintain that all these characterizations suggest that silence in the primeval sense of the un*concealedness* of beyng is the abyssal-ground of the sounding and sound, which emerge as the rending of silence, in beyng's *un*concealedness.

Given that the word is the clearing as well as the saying and saga of beyng, it follows that Heidegger declares decisive that "the essence of the *sound* and of *sounding* belong to *saga.*"[56] At the same time, he repeatedly characterizes the word as the silence of beyng.[57] I maintain that this characterization implies that the word as saying, saga, and clearing is the silent disclosure of beyng that grounds language as the sonorous saying, as the saying in word-sounds that names beings as beings. In my view, this implication further suggests that the silence of the word is the primordial silence, the unconcealedness of beyng that grounds the essence, and this means—is the origin, of language. Silence and its rending would thus unfold in the relation, which Heidegger asserts throughout the course, of the word to beyng and its truth.[58] It is in this vein that he inscribes the human being into such relation as freedom in the sense of being available for appropriation and "[b]elonging-to *in the truth of being* [des Seyns]"; this belonging-to is itself "hearkening as *silencing*" and the truth of beyng takes the form of the "[a]bysmal-grounding re-fusal."[59]

The following figure summarizes the relations between the different forms of silence, language, and truth:

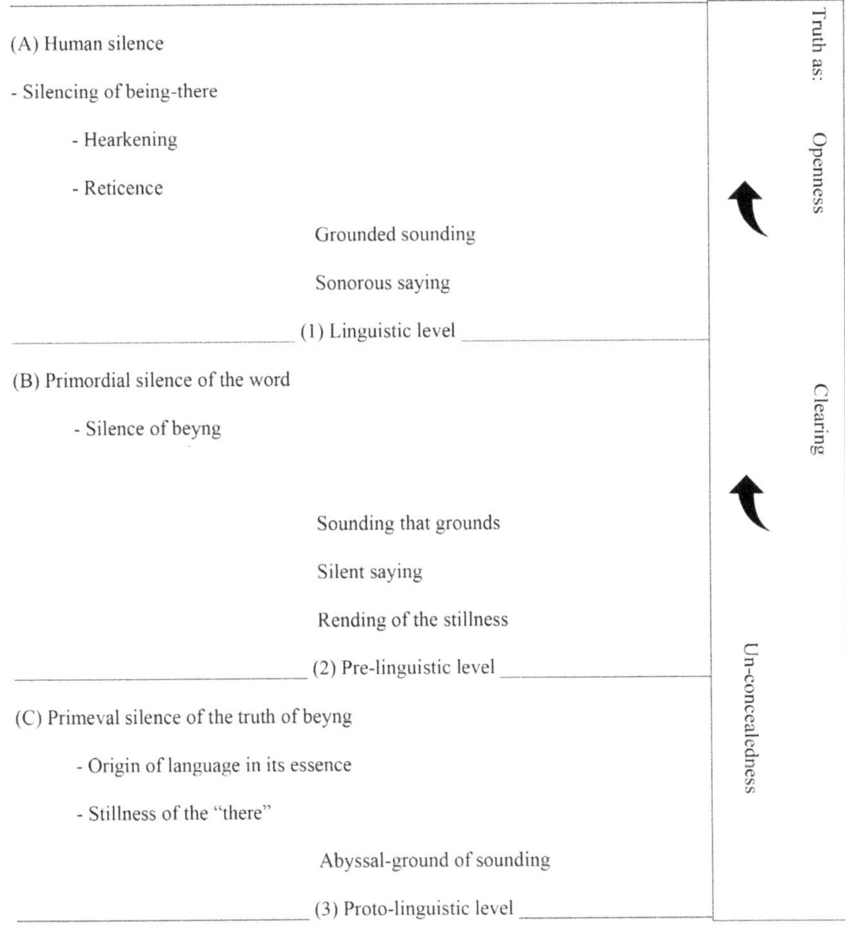

Figure 5.1

We find further confirmation to my inferences concerning silence in his readings of Stephan George's poems, which serve as a bridge—from and back to Herder—for thinking in the crossing. In the student notes that accompany Heidegger's lecture notes, there are various references to the problem of how Herder "crosses" from the inner to the outer language. There are also student notes on how hearing has the character of "crossing" that brings the human being into its freestandingness in the clearing.[60] Heidegger characterizes the sense of hearing in Herder as well in terms of "the manner of *crossing over.*"[61] I maintain that these meanings of "crossing" point to the transcendence of being-there in its silencing and they ultimately converge into the predominant meaning of crossing as the movement from metaphysics toward the leap into being-historical thinking. Heidegger thus turns the direction of the course from the philosophy of language in relation to Herder to the crossing in George's poems.

Heidegger asserts that it is "only through poesy itself and indeed not any, but [a] single one" that being-historical thinking can "ground [language] back in the word."[62] Obviously, he is referring to Hölderlin—"[*the*] *poet of decision*" in whose poetry "the word is already said," but has no "listeners" and thus requires "thinkers."[63] So, George's poems have a propaedeutic role, in "preparation" for "the decision" toward the "other beginning."[64] In Heidegger's view, these poems reflect a "knowledge of the crossing," but it is "too weak and confused."[65] In these poems, we hear the "word of being [*des Seyns*], but veiled and at first word of being-there and also this not a thinking."[66] Therefore, they count as "crossing word," though the poet "speaks barely intimating it, in the manner of crossing."[67] Heidegger thus sets out to appropriate the poet's intimations regarding the word and silence for the thinking in the crossing.

Heidegger's interpretation of George's poem "The Word" focuses on the last stanza of the poem: "No thing may be where the word does break." His reading highlights the disclosive power of the word in its primordial "*naming*" of beings as beings: "The word first lets a being be a being." At the same time, he points to the "ambiguity of the essence of the word" here, which names beings and is the "word of being [*des Seyns*]." Heidegger centers on the latter meaning in accordance with the (transformative, rupturing, and probing) principles of thinking in the crossing. In this light, the breaking of the word is the "refusal" in which "*being* [*das* Seyn] denies itself." I maintain that this characterization means that beyng withdraws into concealedness. As Heidegger puts it here, it is the refusal "of the abysmal-ground on the appropriating-event of deliverance." Such refusal takes the form of silence, more specifically, of the "silencing silence." This is the primeval silence of beyng, which "reigns" over the word, silencing the word.[68]

I maintain that the word is thereby the "tuning 'voice'"of the silence of beyng; it is the *silent* voice of beyng. At the same time, beyng "reveals itself in its refusal—as silence, as 'in between,' as there," that is, in its withdrawal into concealedness. The 'as' of this revelation is crucial: Beyng reveals itself *as* silence in the word, in which "no thing may be," in which no being may be disclosed when the word breaks off. In this light, it is evident that the silence of beyng and the silence of the word are not linguistic silences; they do not unfold within language. Rather, insofar as beyng is the abyssal-ground and the word is the essential origin of language, the silences are primeval and primordial (at the proto-linguistic and pre-linguistic levels), respectively. The experience of these silences, as related in the poem, brings us into "essence-nearness." However, Heidegger seems to part ways here with the poet by rejecting the characterization of the experience in terms of a sad renunciation; there is "no '*forsaking.*'"[69]

In conclusion, the deeper forms of silence that are adumbrated in Heidegger's interpretation of George and in his confrontation with Herder (the primeval silence that belongs to the stillness of beyng and the primordial silencing that belongs to the word), and especially their relation to the truth of beyng and its essencing, remain elusive throughout the course. The silencing in hearkening is traced in bolder lines, though its relation to truth is not as defined. However, this course on the essence of language ends with the question, "And 'language' and its essence and unessence hitherto?" I claim that this is an ending that points to yet another beginning in the pursuit of the question concerning the essence of language. It is fitting that the question concerning silence remains open as well. As Heidegger suggests in the final section of the course titled "The experience of the word," this experience requires "the journey into the attunement and mood," which is that of the insistent hearkening, for "in the silencing intonation of the word—the insistence in the clearing executes itself."[70]

NOTES

1. Martin Heidegger, *On the Essence of Language. The Metaphysics of Language and the Essencing of the Word. Concerning Herder's Treatise* On the Origin of Language, trans. Wanda Torres Gregory and Yvonne Unna (Albany, New York: State University of New York Press, 2004), 3–5 / GA85, 3–5.

2. Ibid., 96 / GA85, 112–13.

3. Ibid., 62 / GA85, 72. For a different view that focuses on Herder's influence on Heidegger, see Peter Hanly, "Marking Silence: Heidegger and Herder on Word and Origin" in *Studia Philosophiae Christianae* Vol. 49, Nr. 4 (2013): 69–86. Hanly argues that Herder was a decisive influence in the development of Heidegger's idea of

language. While Hanly and I agree in viewing Heidegger's engagement with Herder in terms of an *Auseinandersetzung*, I focus on Heidegger's critique of Herder as the setting for his own ideas in the confrontation.

4. Ibid., 4–5 / GA85, 4–5; 45 / GA85, 54; 70 / GA85, 65; 83 / GA85, 97.

5. Cf. ibid., 36 / GA85, 45; 45 / GA85, 54; 70–71 / GA85, 80–81; 83 / GA85, 97; 131–34 / GA85, 153–57; 149 / GA85, 179; 167–74 / GA85, 205–15.

6. Cf. ibid., 3–5 / GA85, 3–5; 29 / GA85, 35.

7. Cf. ibid., 4 / GA85, 4; 18 / GA85, 21; 29 / GA85, 35; 43 / GA85, 51; 55 / GA85, 65; 70 / GA85, 81. Cf. Johann Gottfried Herder, "Essay on the Origin of Language" in *On the Origin of Language. Two Essays by Jean-Jacques Rousseau and Johann Gottfried Herder*, trans. Alexander Gode (New York: Frederick Ungar Publishing Company, 1966), 121.

8. Cf. ibid., 43 / GA85, 51; 123 / GA85, 143.

9. See, for example, ibid., 13 / GA85, 17; 15–16 / GA85, 18–19; 126 / GA85, 146–47.

10. Cf. ibid., 35 / GA85, 43; 71 / GA85, 82.

11. Cf. ibid., 3–4 / GA85, 3–4; 55 / GA85, 65.

12. Cf. ibid., 31 / GA85, 38; 36 / GA85, 45; 43 / GA85, 51; 55 / GA85, 65; 70 / GA85, 81.

13. Ibid., 127 / GA85, 148.

14. Ibid., 16 / GA85, 19.

15. Ibid., 123 / GA85, 143. Cf. ibid., 17 / GA85, 21.

16. Cf. ibid., 15–17 / GA85, 18–21; 28, GA84, 34; §28.

17. Ibid., 3 / GA85, 3.

18. Cf. ibid., 6–8 / GA85, 7–9; 13–14 / GA85, 16–17; 24 / GA85, 28–29; 29 / GA85, 36; 37–38 / GA85, 45–47; 65–66 / GA85, 75–76.

19. Cf. ibid., 19 / GA85, 23; 23 / GA85, 28.

20. Ibid., 24 / GA85, 28.

21. Ibid., 29 / GA85, 35. A student (Siegfried Bröse) captures the gist of Heidegger's claim here: "And so Herder appears to remain in what is animalistic because he thinks from the beginning within the animal economy" (ibid., 145 / GA85, 173–74).

22. One of Heidegger's students (Karl Ulmer) summarizes this argument (ibid., 167 / GA85, 205).

23. Cf. ibid., 30 / GA85, 37; 38–39 / GA85, 48; 46–47 / GA85, 56; 133 / GA85, 156; 139 / GA85, 164; 141 / GA85, 167.

24. Cf. ibid., 29 / GA85, 35l; 46–47 / GA85, 56; 157 / GA85, 134.

25. Cf. ibid., 5 / GA85, 6; 18–19 / GA85, 22–23; 70 / GA85, 65.

26. Ibid., 5 / GA85, 6.

27. Ibid., 46 / GA85, 56.

28. Heidegger later makes these connections more explicit: "The essence of freedom—from essence of the truth of being [*des Seyns*]; from the same abysmal-ground: the essence of the word" (ibid., 65 / GA85, 75).

29. Ibid., 3/ GA85, 3. Cf. Herder, "Essay on the Origin of Language," 87.

30. Ibid., 29–30 / GA85, 36. Cf. ibid., 77 / GA85, 89; 135 / GA65, 159.

31. Ibid., 73 / GA85, 85.

32. Herder, "Essay on the Origin of Language," 49, 63.

33. Heidegger, *On the Essence of Language. The Metaphysics of Language and the Essencing of the Word. Concerning Herder's Treatise* On the Origin of Language, 79 / GA85, 92.

34. Cf. ibid., 65–66 / GA85, 75–76; 120 / GA85, 138–39.

35. Ibid., 55 / GA85, 65.

36. Ibid., 66 / GA85, 76. Cf. ibid., 77 / GA85, 89.

37. Ibid., 108 / GA85, 128.

38. Ibid., 120 / GA85, 139.

39. Ibid., 96 / GA85, 113.

40. Ibid., 108 / GA85, 128.

41. Ibid., 6 / GA85, 8.

42. Ibid., 46 / GA85, 55. Cf. ibid., 18 / GA85, 22; 28–29 / GA85, 35; 128 / GA85, 149. Herder's notion of the mark as functioning between non-sonorous representation and sonorous expression is for Hanly a key point of influence in Heidegger—in the "crossing" from the "metaphysical opposition of sound and silence by virtue of its functioning *between*" and in "the listening that gathers around what he calls a 'clearing'. . . as 'mark,' but as mark that *carries silence in and as its breaking*" (Hanly, "Marking Silence: Heidegger and Herder on Word and Origin," 83). Hanly seems to be conflating the silencing of hearkening with the silencing of the word as clearing, which indeed "carries silence in and as its breaking." Furthermore, given Heidegger's critique of the very concept of "mark," my sense is that "saying" in the pregnant sense of "disclosing" beyng and "naming" beings as beings is a more suitable term.

43. Ibid., 119 / GA85, 137.

44. Ibid., 55 / GA85, 65.

45. Ibid., 80 / GA85, 93.

46. Ibid., 96 / GA85, 113.

47. Ibid., 93–94 / GA85, 109–110.

48. Ibid., 94 / GA85, 110.

49. Ibid., 18 / GA85, 22.

50. Ibid., 28 / GA85, 35.

51. Ibid., 45 / GA85, 54.

52. Ibid., 107 / GA85, 125. Cf. ibid., 113 / GA85, 132.

53. Ibid., 93 / GA85, 109.

54. Ibid., 102 / GA85, 118.

55. Ibid., 109 / GA85, 128. Even more categorically, but also more cryptically, Heidegger draws arrows that seem to connect "Sound and ring—" with the "peal of silence" or stillness and with the "ring-ing (*Er-klingen*) of the silence," and also seem to link the "peal of silence" itself with "the sounding that is *completely different*" (ibid., 78 / GA85, 90).

56. Ibid., 114 / GA85, 133. The history-grounding character of the word is also suggested in its role as "the saga" of beyng (ibid., 73 / GA85, 85). Cf. ibid., 46 / GA85, 55.

57. Cf. ibid., 28 / GA85, 34–35; 66 / GA85, 76; 77 / GA85, 89–90; 102 / GA85, 118; 128 / GA85, 149.

58. Cf. ibid., 5 / GA85, 5; 55 / GA85, 65; 65 / GA85, 75; 128 / GA85, 149.

59. Ibid., 65–66 / GA85, 75–76.

60. Cf. ibid., 154–57 / GA85, 186–90; 164 / GA85, 200.

61. Ibid., 105 / GA85, 123.

62. Ibid., 47 / GA85, 57.

63. Ibid., 4–5 / GA85, 4–5.

64. Ibid., 47 / GA85, 57.

65. Ibid., 51 / GA85, 61.

66. Ibid., 59 / GA85, 69.

67. Ibid., 62 / GA85, 72. Heidegger later returns to George's poem and explicitly renders (unqualified) positive interpretations in two of the essays of *On the Way to Language*. In "Words," the poem serves as a springboard for his focus on the bestowal of presence in language as saying that shows. In "The Nature of Language," he focuses on the clearing-concealing of language in the fourfold and the ringing of stillness. See Heidegger, *On the Way to Language,* trans. Peter D. Hertz (New York: Harper & Row, 1971).

68. Ibid., 61–62 / GA85, 72. Cf. ibid., 46 / GA85, 55.

69. Ibid., 62 / GA85, 72. Perhaps, he is also suggesting that the silencing of hearkening is required for this experience to become a "tuning voice of being-there" by simply concluding his discussion of George's poetry with the poem "Listen to what the somber earth speaks" (ibid. 59 / GA85, 69).

70. Ibid., 128 / GA85, 149.

Chapter 6

Toward the Originary Logic of Silence in a Translation of Heraclitus

In the 1944 summer seminar "Logic: Heraclitus's Doctrine of the *Logos*," Heidegger makes the preliminary remark that the aim of the course is "to arrive at an originary logic," which he defines as "the thinking 'of the' *Logos*," and critically distinguishes from the logic of metaphysics throughout his lectures.[1] The seminar ends with a numbered list of guidelines for this thinking that would meditate on and belong to the *Logos*. Some of the directives for that originary logic suggest an intricate conception of silence that is reflected in the elaborate use of terms related to "*schweigen*" and "*das Schweigen*," with cognates such as "*Beschweigen*," "*Erschweigen*," "*Verschweigung*," and "*Zu-schweigen*." The obscure play of words hints at different layers and forms of silence that I aim to expose in this chapter.

Looking at the broader context first, we see that a year before, in the 1943 summer seminar "The Inception of Occidental Thinking," Heidegger identifies Heraclitus as an inceptual thinker who is called "The Obscure" precisely because his thinking is attuned to the obscure as such, that is, to the *krupthesthai* of *physis*, which Heidegger interprets as the self-concealing of being. I claim that the connection between self-concealing and silence subtly traverses what Heidegger defines here as the project of an authentic thinking of what is "the to-be-thought" in Heraclitus.

On one hand, Heidegger characterizes Heraclitus as the thinker whose life and saying are both marked by a godly silence. The stories that place Heraclitus near the oven in his humble abode or playing with children by the temple of Artemis, for example, point to the presencing of the gods, about whom one should be reticent: "It is better not to speak too much, too loudly or too often about the gods."[2] The presencing of the gods, as exemplified in Apollo, who "neither reveals (*legein*) nor conceals (*kruptei*), but gives signs (*semainei*)," is also soundless in some way, insofar as giving signs is a more originary form of revealing-concealing that points to what is concealed.[3] Heraclitus's word is itself protected by Artemis and comes "from out of the inceptually soundless word that itself remains intact."[4] According to Heidegger, it is no less significant that the goddess personifies *physis*, which the ancient Greeks understood as pure emerging, and Heraclitus thought in its essential relation to self-concealing.

On the other hand, Heidegger defines his own task of trans*lating* Heraclitus as a trans*porting* of his originary word. As with every translation it is an "interpretation" that is "unexpressed," or "carried out silently."[5] This interpretation lays out as well what is "not named inceptually" and "remains the unsaid and still unsayable" in Heraclitus's saying: *alētheia* as the essence of *physis,* the unconcealedness of the pure emerging that is self-concealing.[6] Heidegger suggests that for naming to be inceptual, it must involve the word "is," "[t]he word of all words, the very ether of language," which "names that in which all saying and silence are suspended." He also points here to the essential role that the word itself plays as the site of disclosure in the determination of what is unsayable: "The sole reason the human being is affected by the un-sayable is because whatever comes into appearance comes from out of the word. The un-sayable would not appear if all appearing did not remain originally interwoven with the sphere of saying and the word."[7] At the close of the seminar, he identifies "the true" with "the unsaid" and proclaims that "we must listen to what is unsaid, to what in the unsaid keeps its silence before us," for "we cannot escape the unsaid in our essence." However, Heidegger does not elaborate on the essential relations between being, truth, saying, and silence that are intimated in these pronouncements. This would require further reflection on another foundational word in Heraclitus: the *Logos*, which Heidegger briefly discusses here as the self-revealing forgathering (*Versammlung*) of the originary oneness of *physis*.[8]

A year later, Heidegger sets out to develop his interpretation of Heraclitus's saying of the *Logos,* and silence itself becomes a theme. In the 1944 seminar, his words on silence mark the conclusion of his interpretative translation of Heraclitus's sayings, that is, of his saying of what Heraclitus says, does not say, and could not say about the *Logos*. I maintain that Heidegger ultimately gives word to his own thinking in terms of the appropriating-event of the truth of beyng in this journey through the said, the unsaid, and the unsayable in Heraclitus. What he says about silence in his retrieval of the pre-metaphysical *Logos* would best fit the categories of the unsaid and the unsayable in Heraclitus. In fact, what Heidegger says about both the *Logos* and silence here will resonate in his later reflections on the essence of language as the peal of the stillness.

Heidegger guides us through three different paths toward answering the question "What is the *Logos*?" in the Heraclitan fragments. In the first path, we gain access to the *Logos* as being, through its identification as the One that unites all that is. The second path prepares us better for listening to what he says about silence. This path takes us through the original meaning of *legein* to give us access to that of the *Logos*. Here, Heidegger argues that *legein* originally had nothing to do with assertion, speech, and language, but instead originally meant "to harvest" and "to gather." As in the harvesting of wine grapes, *legein* involves a host of activities oriented toward preserving and conserving, which as a whole presuppose a self-gathering and a considered forgathering in their orientation. Understanding the essence of *legein* gives us access to the *Logos* as the harvest and the forgathering, which is "the originary forgathering that safeguards beings as the beings that they are," it is "being itself, within which all beings unfold."[9] I claim that, because harvesting and the harvest, gathering and the originary forgathering, are not properly linguistic, but instead ground what is linguistic, it is likely that all of this must occur in a silence that is deeper than speech and language.

The third path sheds a little more light in preparation for what Heidegger does say about silence. This path grants us access to the *Logos* through the *logos* of the *psyche*, that is, of the human being, who is in the manner of harvesting and gathering, and is thereby defined in its essence in the originary relation with the harvest and the originary forgathering. *Homologein* is the concordance (*Einklang*) of the *Logos* of being and the human *logos*. The proper concordance requires that the human hearken to and say the same as being, but this is difficult. Though being presences toward the human and the human is pointed toward being, being absences at the same time and the human forgets being in its sojourn in the midst of beings.[10]

Heidegger explains that in the forgetting of being, "[h]uman listening does not easily gather itself toward the *Logos*: rather, tends to run astray and disperse itself in such a way that it predominantly listens to human speech and human utterance."[11] I maintain that hearkening to the *Logos,* in contrast, involves listening to and obeying the silent address of being. Heidegger correspondingly assigns a special role in this hearkening to the *Logos* in Heraclitus, who "had to bring to word something that was once unsaid and never fully sayable."[12]

Moreover, what Heidegger calls the "exemplary *legein*" and the "[a]uthentic knowledge that consists of attentive listening to the *Logos,*" which are possible only in "thoughtful and poetic saying," are also marked by silences.[13] In this vein, Heidegger points to "the human who is appropriate to beyng" as one who "is quiet and speaks with it."[14] As with Heraclitus, not only can such sayings be reticent in their response, but also, and more fundamentally, they are determined by a silence that draws limits on what can be said.

Heidegger suggests that the Greek inceptual thinkers, including Heraclitus, did not name *alētheia* inceptually because they could not. They named the "essential oneness" of *alētheia* understood as unconcealedness and *physis* understood as emerging. They also named the essential determination of *legein* as gathering "from out of *alethea* (i.e., the unconcealed and its revealed)." However, they "did not specifically name" the "covering-over" that unfolds in *alētheia.* More fundamentally, they did not think the essence of *alētheia* as the unconcealedness of being. Presumably, here the concealedness of being itself and the forgetful focus on what is unconcealed, that is, on beings, rules in the "omission and failure of enunciation."[15] Thus, I claim that silence has key roles with regard to the essence of *alētheia* and to the sayings of *alētheia* as well.

Heidegger states that the truth of beyng itself has not yet "come into its word."[16] I maintain that this silence would also hold sway over the possibility of enunciating the "originary relatedness" of the *Logos* and the human *logos.* In this regard, Heidegger asserts that neither the Greeks, nor even Heraclitus, nor anybody yet has had the "proper word and . . . proper saying" for that primordial relation. The guidelines that he offers when he speaks about silence are thus for the *Logos* which "has yet to unfold inceptually."[17]

Turning now to the guidelines for the originary logic, we find that Heidegger explicitly characterizes the originary relation between the *Logos* and the human *logos* in terms of silence or quiescence. Beginning at the layer of *legein,* the gathering that secures beings, Heidegger says, "The human—quiescent, at first, in regard to the being of beings—per-ceives beings in their being, and therefore beings as such." He calls this form of silence "*Be-schweigen des Seins,*" which has been translated as "ac-quiescence to being," possibly to convey the quiet acceptance of the being of beings in per-ceiving. Heidegger identifies it as "the originary saying and naming of beings."[18] We can infer that it is silent insofar as it is not a linguistic expression in word-sounds; rather, it is the "originary word," from which speech as saying and naming in word-sounds originate. In this sense, I maintain that the ac-quiescence to being is at the pre-linguistic level.

There is a more fundamental sense in which the originary saying and naming of beings is silent: It does not say or name being. To say is essentially to show; to name is essentially to point; both involve letting something be seen or disclosing it as something.[19] *Legein* as the gathering that secures beings lets them be seen or discloses them as beings. So, my contention is that in the ac-quiescence to being, being itself withdraws and remains concealed as the human focuses on what is unconcealed.

I propose that if we translate "*Be-schweigen des Seins*" more literally as "be-silencing of being," we can capture the crucial sense in which it is at the same time an active and permeating silence that belongs to being itself in its concealedness. What Heidegger calls "*Beschweigen*" belongs to the human *logos* and to the *Logos* of being in their originary relation. This is why he states that acquiescence "unfolds as the originary self-gathering of the human essence toward being, and vice versa," that is, of being toward the human essence, of the *Logos* toward the human *logos*.[20]

In my reading, acquiescence is the more originary pre-linguistic silence from which speech as gathering in word-sounds originates. From this perspective, there would also be a sense in which acquiescence is reflected within speech itself. This would be the silence that unfolds sonorously, linguistically. It permeates the fundamental word "is," which the human is able to apply to beings in its quiescent per-ceiving of being.[21] It also permeates the quiet response to the *Logos*, the hearkening and reticent concordance of thoughtful and poetic sayings with the silent address of being.

Heidegger not only characterizes *legein* as the harvesting that secures beings in terms of its "quiet" enactment but also identifies it both as "the gathered gathering of the self-abiding quiescence" and as "originary quiescence." This originary silence that rests in itself is what enables us to relate to beings as such, in what Heidegger here calls "the entire self-comportment of the human to beings."[22] I claim that it is on the basis of such self-comportment that we are able to speak to and about beings in sonorous words. If *legein* is the harvesting and the gathering of beings that conserves and preserves them as beings, then the saying and naming of beings in speech is the reaping in word-sounds of what is silently sown. Such reaping has the possibility of being silent as well in the hearkening and reticent sayings of thinkers and poets.

The silences that are enacted in the human *logos*—the ac-quiescence to being and the quiet concordance with being—are possibilities that lie in the essence of the human in its openness to being. However, I maintain that these are possibilities that are themselves grounded in *legein*, the originary silence. Moreover, the originary relatedness of the human *logos* to the *Logos* brings us to deeper silences that, for Heidegger, have their ground in being and its truth. We can see him taking this direction when he points to the fact that "what applies to *legein*" as acquiescence "applies in an even more originary way to the *Logos*." The reason that he gives introduces another form of quiescence here: The *Logos* is "the originary securing requiescence (*Verschweigung*)."[23] So, if the *Logos* is the forgathering of being within which beings emerge as beings, then requiescence is the silence of being within which beings rest, safeguarded as beings.

In my interpretation, requiescence operates at the proto-linguistic level, for it is what enables language in its essence to unfold, and it is a primeval silence. The *Logos* in its originary securing requiescence, according to Heidegger, is "as such the fore-word," it is "not the word," but "the foreword to any language, more originary than the word."[24] This would mean that the *Logos* is the silent fore-word that secures what is unconcealed in the unconcealedness of being. Language in its essence is the word, it is the gathering and harvesting of what is unconcealed in the saying and naming that become sonorous in speech. So, my sense is that there can be no word-sounds without the word and there can be no word without the fore-word.

Heidegger introduces more terms related to quiescence in his characterization of the fore-word: "The fore-word is the acquieting of the stillness that unfolds in advance and before the essence of the word."[25] The verbal sense of "*Erschweigen*," which is translated as "acquieting," suggests an active silence, a silencing that is a concealing. I claim that the stillness is the quiet and the repose of the original concealedness; it is the deepest (primeval) silence. In this sense, acquieting could only have its essence as a concealing silencing from the stillness itself.

The stillness as the deepest quiescence is deeper than requiescence—what I have identified as the silence of being, because it concerns the *truth* of being. Heidegger seems to suggest as much when he claims "the truth of being shelters itself in the stillness of what was always already there in advance." He also uses terms here that evoke the stillness when he characterizes the truth of being here as preserving the "tranquility" of the appropriating-event, which "eventuates itself in order to let all that exists rest upon it."[26]

Truth as *un*concealedness involves a wresting away from concealedness. I claim that a similar wresting away occurs with regard to the stillness, which Heidegger says, "must be broken only when the word is to be."[27] The word as the saying that becomes sonorous in speech would thus break out into unconcealedness from the stillness of the original concealedness, that is, from the deepest silence. However, the stillness should not be conceived in negative terms, that is, as an absence of sounds. Instead, it should be conceived in positive terms. I would argue that it is the originary source from which all other forms of silence draw their essence. I would also argue that it is the site from which the very dif-ference (*Unter-Schied*) between what is and what is not sonorous with regard to speech can emerge.

Heidegger introduces yet another term related to quiescence. The term is "*Zu-schweigen*," which translated literally is a "silencing-to." It has been translated as "quiet sending," perhaps to capture the verbal force of "*schweigen*" as well as the sense of directionality of the "*zu*," by rendering it figuratively as a sending. This form of silence pertains to the relation of the *Logos* to the human *logos*, of being to the human. Heidegger says that the *Logos* "quietly sends being to the human." Since he also characterizes this quiet sending here as a "speaking-toward and a speaking-to," my claim is that it is the silent address of being to the human.[28]

I would also argue that the quiet sending arises out of what Heidegger calls the "need" of being for "*legein*" and for "securement in the humanness of the human." Such need takes here the form of a "demand" that being "makes upon the essence of the human." Put differently, the harvest needs the harvesting, claims for the harvester, and thereby defines the harvester as such. Once again, we can link the silent character of the address to the concealing of being itself in the unconcealing of beings as beings. This seems to be what Heidegger himself has in mind here when he claims: "The truth of being . . . quietly sends itself to the human." He also refers to this quiet sending here in terms of the truth of beyng that "calls to the human essence."[29] It is insofar as the human receives and responds to this call, that the human is the "safekeeper of the truth of beyng."[30] In the same vein, he points to *Ereignis* as what "surpasses being and the human in their relatedness" insofar as "prior to them both," it "eventuates into truth as the securing of concealment and its essencing." Presumably, such concealment and its essencing are harbored in the deepest silence that belongs to the stillness to which beyng returns in its withdrawal: "In stillness, beyng turns toward the concealing of the clearing."[31]

In conclusion, Heidegger's use of terms related to *schweigen* obscurely suggest a very complex interplay regarding silence:

There are different players:

(A) The *Logos* or being in its forgathering;
(B) The human *logos* in its gathering; and
(C) *Alētheia* as unconcealedness—or, ultimately, the truth of beyng in the event.

Quiescence takes on multiple forms as well, according to what is at play:

(1) The human ac-quiescence to the *Logos*;
(2) The quiet concordance of the human *logos* with the *Logos*;
(3) The acquiescence that characterizes the originary relatedness of the *Logos* and the human *logos*;
(4) The more originary quiescence of *legein*;
(5) The originary requiescence of the *Logos*;
(6) The acquieting of the *Logos* as foreword;
(7) The quiet sending of being from the *Logos* to the human; and, finally,
(8) The stillness in which the truth of beyng shelters itself.

The increasing depth reflected in the list, which ends with the stillness to which belongs the deepest silence, suggests the idea of quiescence as an organic whole. We can apply Heidegger's definition of the *Logos* as the harvest to capture this point: The stillness corresponds to the stage of germination, the various forms of quiescence of the *Logos* in relation to the human *logos* correspond to various stages of sprouting and blooming, the human ac-quiescence to the stage of sowing, and the possibilities of silence in saying and in the word-sounds of speech correspond to the stage of reaping.

In my reading of Heidegger's words, I have interpreted quiescence in its close association with concealedness, following clues in his remarks on the relation between *alētheia* and *legein* and his hints concerning the truth of beyng. However, it is important to note that the dynamism of unconcealedness as a whole—the emergence of beings, the presencing and absencing of being, and its wresting away from and returning to concealedness—is reflected in the various ways that silence unfolds. I claim that each form of quiescence has its way of silencing and each in turn characterizes a form of disclosive gathering. The vibrancy of concealedness—in its sheltering of all the originary temporal possibilities of being—is reflected in the stillness as well, in the sense that it stills all that rests in it as the quietest repose.

Intent on rejecting the metaphysical and common interpretation of *logos* in terms of assertion, saying, language, or speech, Heidegger does not pursue the question as to how the original meaning of gathering came to have these meanings. In fact, he states that it is "perhaps" an "unfitting" question, presumably because it concerns the metaphysical *logos*.[32] However, he does suggest that there may be a way of showing how the common meaning of the German "*lesen*" (reading) originates from gathering.[33] Similarly, he states that Kant's metaphysical determination of thinking as a connecting shows a "faint shimmer of the originary essence of *legein*."[34] At the same time, Heidegger's more "fitting" reflection on the inceptual *Logos* intimates that the silent forgathering and unconcealedness of being are the originary forces at play in the emergence of language in its essence and of speech as such.

My contention is that the different kinds of quiescence take on different forms in relation to what is linguistic as well. Following this clue, I have identified the silences that are at the linguistic level, as in the reticent sayings of thinkers and poets. Other forms of silence seem to play a primordial grounding role. These are the silences that I have identified at the pre-linguistic level, the silences from which speech can emerge (1–4 in the list above). There are also the silences at the proto-linguistic level, from which the word, language in its essence, can emerge (5–8). These forms of quiescence, which seem to have an originative role, include the silences of the fore-word and the deepest silence that is the stillness. The general sense, then, is that language has its multilayered ground and ultimate origin in quiescence.

The sonorous dimension of what is linguistic, that is, the saying and naming in word-sounds that occurs in speech, has its ground in soundlessness. The deepest soundlessness is that of the stillness, a silence that must be broken for the word as such to be. In fact, Heidegger extends the relation between sound and soundlessness, and he broadens its scope beyond linguistic sounds. He argues that not only is hearkening fundamentally different from listening as acoustic perception in general, but it is also the "originary listening," without which acoustic listening would not be possible. In this sense, he claims that we "have ears because we can listen in a hearkening way."[35] Our ability to hear sounds as particular sounds, say, as the tones of the harp (to use one of his own examples), is thus based ultimately on our openness to the soundless and inaudible voice of being.

As I will later show, Heidegger's concept of the peal of the stillness, which he develops in the 1950s, retains many of the positive, vibrant, and originative characteristics of silence that I have identified in his guidelines for an originary logic. However, this pursuit of the inceptual *Logos* eventually takes explicit form as the thinking of the truth of beyng that seeks to undergo the experience of the essence of language. The fourfold of earth, sky, mortals, and immortals and the waying of the world will take a central role in the peal of the stillness and the dynamics of silence overall.

Two other essays on Heraclitus, which are based on the two seminars that I have examined here, offer a preliminary view into some of the modifications in Heidegger's reading of Heraclitus: In "*Alētheia* (Heraclitus, Fragment 16)," which was delivered in the year of the 1943 seminar and published in 1951, Heidegger issues the new claim that in Heraclitus, "*Logos* is in itself and at the same time a revealing and a concealing. It is *Alētheia*."[36] This direct identification of *Logos* with *Alētheia* does not occur in either seminar. The closest Heidegger gets to suggesting it is in the 1944 seminar, where he states that in the Greeks, the *Logos* is in an "originary relation to *alētheia*," so that *legein* as gathering "gets its essence" from out of *alethea*, from what has been gathered from out of concealedness and forgathered into unconcealedness or revealing.[37]

In "*Logos* (Heraclitus, Fragment 50)," which was delivered in the year of the 1944 seminar and published in 1951, Heidegger advances the statement that neither Heraclitus nor "all the Greeks after him—thought the essence of language as *Logos*, as the Laying that gathers," and therefore did not think "the essence of language from the essence of Being."[38] This statement is concordant with the claim made in the 1944 seminar that neither the Greeks nor anybody has the "proper word and . . . proper saying" for the primordial relation between the *Logos* and the human *logos*.[39] However, it is evidently framed in terms of Heidegger's question concerning the essence of language.

The modifications in Heidegger's formulations concerning the ancient Greek *Logos* in his trans-lations of Heraclitus suggest that what he says about the *Logos* will later resonate in his own concept of the essence of language in terms of the peal of the stillness. However, it is especially noteworthy that Heidegger does not explicitly broach the topic of silence in either of the Heraclitus essays. In the next chapter, we will see him turn to silence in the context of his reflections on the essence of language, when we will hear echoes of his originary logic of quiescence.

NOTES

1. Martin Heidegger, *Heraclitus. The Inception of Occidental Thinking and Logic: Heraclitus's Doctrine of the* Logos, trans. Julia Goesser Assaiante and S. Montgomery Ewegen (London: Bloomsbury Academic, 2018), 139 / GA55, 185.
2. Ibid., 20 / GA55, 24.
3. Ibid., 134 / GA55, 178.
4. Ibid., 21 / GA55, 27.
5. Cf. ibid., 37 / GA55, 59; 49 / GA55, 63.
6. Cf. ibid., 131 / GA55, 174; Martin Heidegger and Eugen Fink, *Heraclitus Seminar*, trans. Charles H. Seiber (Evanston: Northwestern University Press, 1994): "We will also have to say for Heraclitus that there is a saying to which the unsaid belongs, but not the unsayable. The unsaid, however, is no lack and no barrier for saying" (52 / GA15, 89).
7. Ibid., 62 / GA55, 82.
8. Ibid., 134–35 / GA55, 178–80.
9. Ibid., 210 / GA55, 278.
10. Ibid., §6.2b.
11. Ibid., 230 / GA55, 306.
12. Ibid., 281 / GA55, 377.
13. Cf. ibid., 246 / GA55, 329; 268 / GA55, 358; 276 / GA55, 370.
14. Ibid., 281 / GA55, 377.
15. Ibid., 272–73 / GA55, 365–66.
16. Ibid., 256–57 / GA55, 345.
17. Ibid., 281 / GA55, 378.
18. Ibid., 285 / GA55, 382.
19. Cf. ibid., 163 / GA55, 215; 295 / GA55, 399.
20. Ibid, 285 / GA55, 382.
21. Ibid., 254 / GA55, 341.
22. Ibid., 285 / GA55, 382–83.
23. Ibid.
24. Ibid.
25. Ibid.
26. Ibid.
27. Ibid.
28. Ibid.
29. Ibid.
30. Ibid., 289 / GA55, 387
31. Ibid., 285 / GA55, 382-83.
32. Ibid., 285 / GA55, 382.
33. Ibid., §5.b.

34. Ibid., 286 / GA55, 384.

35. Ibid., 189 / GA55, 247. Cf. ibid., 198 / GA55, 260.

36. Heidegger, "*Alētheia* (Heraclitus, Fragment 16)" in *Early Greek Thinking*, trans. David Ferrell Krell and Frank A. Capuzzi (New York: Harper & Row, 1974), 71 / GA7, 213.

37. Heidegger, *Heraclitus. The Inception of Occidental Thinking and Logic: Heraclitus's Doctrine of the* Logos, 272–75 / GA55, 364–67.

38. Heidegger, "*Logos* (Heraclitus, Fragment 50)" in *Early Greek Thinking*, 77–8 / GA7, 220–21.

39. Heidegger, *Heraclitus. The Inception of Occidental Thinking and Logic: Heraclitus's Doctrine of the* Logos, 256–57 / GA55, 345.

Chapter 7

Quiet Musings in the Project toward the Stillness

Volume 74 of Heidegger's *Gesamtausgabe, Zum Wesen der Sprache und Zur Frage nach der Kunst* (*On the Essence of Language and On the Question Concerning Art*) contains some of Heidegger's previously unpublished thoughts on the essence of language and on art dating from the late 1930s to 1960. His fragmentary musings on silence appear throughout this work in both prose and poetic form. In section 7.1, I focus on his words as a thinker, and in section 7.2, I follow his role of the thinker as the poet.

7.1. THE WORDS OF THE THINKER

My discussion of Heidegger's words as a thinker on the stillness and its silencing here concentrates mostly on two sections: 119. "Die Erschweigung der Stille" (The Silencing of the Stillness) and 149. "Das Erschweigen der Stille" (Silencing of the Stillness), which following the editor's prefatory descriptions, seem to have been written after his 1939 summer seminar on Herder. I maintain that in these sections, which together amount to a few short and fragmentary paragraphs, Heidegger sketches out his thoughts on silence, particularly in its primeval relation to beyng itself in the appropriating-event and as thc origin of the essence of language. As my analysis will show, the connections between the forms of silence, language as saying, and truth as unconcealedness are quite intricate. Heidegger offers a terminological distinction that may be helpful for unraveling the highly nuanced understanding of silence that is suggested in his few and reserved words.

The three words that Heidegger distinguishes are the substantivized infinitives "*Verschweigen*," "*Schweigen*," and "*Erschweigen*." The verb "*verschweigen*" commonly means to keep secret, to withhold, hide, or conceal something; the noun "*Verschweigung*" means silence, in the sense of suppressing or concealing something; and "*Verschwiegenheit*" means secrecy, reticence, or reserve. In Heidegger's rendition, "*Verschweigen*," which I translate here as "keeping secret," means "not to say something sayable . . . not to share and this furthermore for different reasons (motives and interests)." "*Das Sagen*" (saying) in Heidegger's lexicon means "*das Zeigen*" (showing or letting something be seen). So, keeping secret means not showing what can be shown. Elsewhere in the text, Heidegger refers to beyng itself in terms of its "*Verschweigung*" or its concealing or veiling silence.[1] Thus, I claim that we can have an initial sense of how keeping silent relates to the hiddenness or concealedness that characterizes truth.

The infinitive "*schweigen*" means to be silent, to say nothing or to be quiet, while the noun "*das Schweigen*" means silence or quiescence. I will translate "*Schweigen*" as being silent. Heidegger characterizes it as "*to want* to say what is unsayable, but to be unable (being silent out of inability), to leave what is unutterable in its unsayability (being silent out of ability)."[2] We enter a deeper and more complex layer of silence, for it pertains to what cannot be shown in a given case. It also arises from two very different dispositions on our part as we encounter what cannot be shown.

"*Das Erschweigen*" (silencing or to silence) and "*die Erschweigung*" (the silencing) are not commonly used terms. We know that it is important for Heidegger that the prefix "*er-*" typically emphasizes the beginning of an action or the end of an action that results in something being affected. In Heidegger's rendition, it concerns "the unsaid—because essentially in all saying what is fore- and with- and after-said [is] in its ground, to keep back the ground of its unsaidness and preserve all saying, in order to conserve it carefully."[3] We have entered a much deeper layer than those of keeping silent and being silent. Silencing pertains to the unsaid, that is, to the unshown. I claim that Heidegger thereby identifies the ground of saying in the unsaid, of showing in the unshown.

The unsaid has a threefold structure (the fore-, the with-, and the after-said), which pertains to what is unsaid at the very moment of saying, to what is unshown at the very moment of showing. I maintain that this structure can be rendered in terms of temporality: the moment of saying is grounded in the futurality, the being-present, and the having-been of what is unsaid. So, in this unified temporal sense, saying has its ground in the always already unsaid. Put otherwise: showing has its ground in the always already unshown. Silencing actively lets this unsaidness or unshownness remain as such, and this has the effect of preserving saying in its showing—in its letting something be seen.[4]

My contention is that there are even deeper layers to silence and to saying or showing, which Heidegger depicts in terms of beyng, the word, and the appropriating-event. He refers to these layers once he reaches the deepest of the human possibilities of silence, that is, of our silencing of what is unsaid. In his words: "This ground of this unsaidness is the abyssal-ground, as the one that beyng itself essences."[5] I claim that this means that beyng—in the withdrawal that characterizes its unconcealedness (from and back to the original concealedness)— determines what is to be the always already unsaid or unshown. Furthermore, this implies that the *un*concealedness of beyng, which involves a wresting away from concealedness, determines the saying that has its ground in unsaidness.

Following my interpretation above, if unsaidness and saying are thus both determined in advance, then language itself as the word of beyng has its origin and determination in the unconcealedness of beyng. Heidegger defines the primordial beginning of the word: the "voice of beyng, which silences in the manner of abyssally-grounding and in the manner of silencing, is the beginning of the word."[6] I maintain that we are at the fourth layer of silence and at a different dimension altogether. The third layer was silence of the unsaid or unshown in *our* saying or in our showing in words, and in this sense it is at the linguistic level. The primordial silencing now described is silence of the unsaid or unshown in saying or showing *as such*, which places it as the pre-linguistic level. This is the form of silence that unfolds in the primordial saying or showing, which is that of the word as the "clearing" of beyng.[7] As the clearing, language in its essence first enables us to speak, and it defines what we can and cannot say, what we can and cannot show in words. Our own possibilities of silence are defined by the essence of language in this sense.

However, I claim that we have not reached the deepest layer of silence with the silencing of the word. Heidegger says, "The word is inceptually the silenced voice of stillness."[8] In my reading, if the word is itself the silenc*ed* voice, then there is a silence that is not only deeper than our words but also deeper than the word itself. The word, that is, language in its essence, in its primordial silencing originates as the voice of stillness. The word as voice says or shows. As silenced voice, it lets the unsaidness remain as such in its saying or showing. As the silenced voice *of stillness*, it belongs to and concerns the stillness.

I maintain that *die Stille* is the fifth layer of silence. We are at yet another dimension, namely, that of the primeval silence that belongs to the stillness. It is the silence beyond the silence of the word, which is its silenced voice. The word itself, the essence of language, has its origin in stillness. So, we are at the proto-linguistic level. Heidegger thus characterizes the stillness of beyng as "the *fore-word*" and "the *first word*."[9] He refers to the stillness itself as "the abyssal-ground of the appropriat-ing event."[10] I claim that this means that the stillness belongs in the withdrawal that characterizes the unconcealedness of beyng. The stillness belongs to the original concealedness; it is the quiet, the calm, the repose of concealedness. If *un*concealedness involves wresting away from concealedness, then there must also be a breaking of the stillness that characterizes concealedness. This breaking of the stillness is what Heidegger calls "the sounding" (*die Lautung*) and describes as a privation of stillness. Sound itself, he emphasizes, *breaks* the stillness, but only as a "rupture" and "breaking-off" of this stillness.[11]

Stillness is commonly defined in negative terms, that is, as the absence or lack of sound or motion, understood as physical processes or objectively present phenomena. Heidegger explicitly rejects the conceptual underpinnings of this "metaphysical" view.[12] The original essence of the word may not be viewed in terms of what is sonorous and of what belongs to what is spoken. I claim that it is in this sense that he refers to the word itself as "the illuminating soundless voice of beyng."[13] He also refers to it as "the soundless voice of the stillness."[14] Moreover, the relationship of the stillness to sounding is not that between what is non-sensible in relationship to what is sensible. This is the sense of his claim that the silent manner in which stillness stills is "not yet a making sound" and of his description of its tuning essence as soundless.[15]

"Soundlessness" or "non-sonorousness" in Heidegger's vocabulary here are not negative concepts. My point is that they do not indicate a lack or an absence. Instead, they indicate a fullness from which sounds as such and what is sonorous as such can eventually emerge.[16] I maintain that this fullness is ultimately that of the stillness, which is marked by the primeval silence, the deepest form in Heidegger's idea of silence. In the beginning, was the stillness, not the word, that is, not language in its essence as the silenced voice of the stillness. The word is itself soundless, but this soundlessness is still derivative, for the word itself has its origin in the stillness.

In my analysis, I discover two kinds of soundlessness that correspond to the two deeper layers of silence. One kind would correspond to the silencing of the word. The other kind would correspond to the deepest layer of silence, that is, to the primeval silence that marks the stillness. We can get a sense of the soundlessness that pertains to the silencing of the word when we consider that language in its essence as the word of beyng is not itself sonorous, for it is the clearing in which our sonorous words can emerge. Heidegger describes this emergence:

> The word has its essence in naming. . . . Naming firstly as appropriat-ing in the silence of the stillness of beyng. Only as silencing can it [naming] break the silence in sound. The word thus becomes word-sound and words thus originate, which however are first gathered and united in the essence of the word.[17]

But the word of beyng originates from what itself is not sonorous either. The essence of language has its origin in the stillness, from which perhaps the very dif-ference between what is sonorous and what is not sonorous can unfold.

Herein would lie the deepest soundlessness, in the primeval calm of the original concealedness out of which the appropriating-event of unconcealedness can bestir all that is onto its eventual resounding in our sonorous words.

In his sparse words, Heidegger thus gives us a glimpse into a quite intricate understanding of silence. It is multilayered—consisting of different forms of silence and at different levels with regard to language as sonorous speech. It is multidimensional—in its relation to our possibilities of silence, to the primordial silence of the word, and to the primeval silence of beyng itself in the appropriating-event. In figure format, silence involves:

(A) Human silence		
- Keeping secret	relates to	something sayable
- Keeping silent	relates to	the unsayable, the unutterable, unsayability
- Silencing	relates to	the unsaid, unsaidness
	(1) Linguistic level	
(B) Primordial silencing of the word	is	the abyssal-ground of unsaidness
		the clearing of beyng
		the silenced voice of the stillness
	(2) Pre-linguistic level	
(C) Primeval silencing of the stillness	is	the first word
		the abyssal-ground of the appropriating-event
	(3) Proto-linguistic level	

Figure 7.1

To my mind, the main strength lies in the vibrant sense that Heidegger gives to silence overall as a positive force. Our possibilities of silence are much more than mere acts of refraining from saying something or of withholding certain words. Both what we say and what we do not say can thus be meaningful ways of disclosing things to others. Each possibility of our silence is a way of relating to something else as well—keeping secret relates to the sayable, keeping silent to the unsayable in a case, and silencing to the unsaid as such. Moreover, these can be positive acts in themselves. Keeping secret can be a way of sheltering what is sayable. Being silent can arise from our ability to leave the unsayable in its unsayability. As for our silencing, it inherently involves the positive acts of preserving and conserving saying with its ground in unsaidness.

Only a mindfulness of the limits of the sayable, the unsayable, and the unsaid, which are marked in the clearing, gives us access to the loftiest possibilities of our silence. I maintain that these concern the deepest layers of silence itself. We can relate in silent ways to the primordial silencing of the word and the primeval silence of the stillness. This requires a hearkening attitude, which demands that we first become silent so that we can hear the deeper silences and listen to their soundlessness. Heidegger thus highlights not only the importance of heeding the limits of the essence of language but also of recognizing that our possibilities of saying and of silence are granted to us, ultimately, in the appropriating-event from the stillness. Beyng itself "has need of" the human essence and thereby addresses the human being in its "calling stillness."[18] Correspondingly, Heidegger offers some guidelines of sigetics for thinking in the crossing. It must recognize that "silenc-ing (*Er-schweigen*) does not originate out of the inadequacy of discourse, but out of the belongingness to the stillness and for it." Here, it must also know that it "may not overcome that which is silenced, because it must be appropriated by that which is silenced."[19]

In conclusion, our possibilities of silence are determined dynamically by the deeper silences that are themselves dynamic, so to speak. The primordial silencing of the word and the primeval silence that belongs to the stillness are vibrant sources that, in Heidegger's rendition, belong to the unconcealedness of beyng and are originating forces of the appropriating-event. The word, as the clearing within which our words and our silences originate, itself actively silenc*es* the unsaid as such in its saying, which also unfolds dynamically as a showing. Moreover, if the stillness belongs in the withdrawal that characterizes the unconcealedness of beyng, then the stillness itself unfolds, so to speak, in that withdrawal. The word arises from the primeval silence of the stillness and the sound breaks off it. So, it is the site out of which the appropriating-event bestirs all that is in the unconcealedness of beyng. The stillness is also active in the sense that it *stills* all that rests in it as the repose of the original concealedness of beyng.[20] Much unfolds in silence, but only an essential experiencing (*Wesenserfahrung*) can give us this insight, for Heidegger claims, "The human being speaks without having an inkling that he thereby breaks the essential silence, which he is not able to know."[21] In the following section, we witness how Heidegger turns to poetry as a form of essential experiencing of silence.

7.2. THE WORDS OF THE THINKER AS POET

In this section, I focus on Heidegger's poem "*Die Geburt der Sprache*" (The Birth of Language), which consists of eight verses and probably dates between 1944 and 1945.[22] It is one of those few instances in which Heidegger plays the role of the thinker as the poet, in consonance with his thoughts on the neighborhood of poetry and thinking. He resumes his part as thinker in the reflections following the poem. Many of the ideas conveyed by his poetic and thinking words reappear in later publications (especially in his interpretations of the poetry of Hölderlin and Trakl), and they anticipate his reflections on the word as the soundless peal of the stillness in the fourfold of the world.

I claim that the poem is "sigetic." As we know from his *Contributions to Philosophy (Of the Event)*, the term has a special meaning for Heidegger. Sigetics, in his definition there, is the mindful "lawfulness" of silencing, which follows the principle that every saying arises from beyng and "speaks *out of* the truth of beyng."[23] In terms of the possibilities of silence discussed in section 7.1, sigetics would include keeping secret, keeping silent, and silencing. Insofar as truth is unconcealedness, the silent saying of sigetics is tuned into the concealedness of beyng itself and thus speaks in the manner of concealing. My main contention is that the stillness—in which belongs the deepest form of the silence of beyng—is concealed in the poem. In this sense, the poem is an attempt to co-respond to the word of beyng as the silent voice of the stillness.

Heidegger's poem as a sigetic saying involves more than reticence and elusiveness. I maintain that in its co-respondence to the secrecy of beyng, it is encrypted for the few who seek the same path. The obscure prose that accompanies it is also sigetic, but the saying of thinking provides some hints for the secret code. In this vein, Heidegger says in prose, "The language that is characteristic of the saying remains in what is unspoken. It can never be spoken directly and brought to understanding on a customary day." Phrasing the sigetic principle quasi-poetically here, he says, "Following in the saying the hints of the word. / Keep clear of the indicating of the wordless terms."[24] I will try to decrypt the poem and what it sigetically says about the stillness. Whether I am transgressing Heidegger's sigetic principles is one of many questions left unanswered in this attempt.

Rendered in prose, the poem alludes to the pre-linguistic and proto-linguistic levels of the sonorous speech of the human being by describing its determinations in terms of a birth. Each of the eight verses of the poem contains a verbal form. Seven begin with a verb (to hint, to sow, to bring, to guard, to build, to call, to presage). This style reflects the vibrant senses of "birth" as an emerging and a bringing-forth. We witness how this dynamic image of birthing unfolds by following the verses in the images that they convey.

The first verse depicts the height as hinting in the greeting of the depth. In my interpretation, this situates the birthing in what Heidegger later calls the fourfold of the world. The height corresponds to the sky, the depth corresponds to the earth.[25] Height and depth establish what he calls in another part of the manuscript the "abiding expanse" (*weilende Weite*). I identify the abiding expanse as the originary time-space that sets the measure and opens the region of their encounter.[26] The hinting of the height suggests the immortals in the sky who silently intimate something to the mortals. The greeting of the depth suggests the immortals in their manner of addressing the mortals on the earth. In the verse, this greeting is soundless, for language has yet to emerge. We seem to be at the proto-linguistic level here, for the essence of language has yet to come forth as well.

The second verse depicts the height again, but as the site from which the seed of the word is sown. I would argue that the depth is present, though it is not mentioned, for the sowing could be said to go from the height to the depth—or in terms of the fourfold, from the hinting immortals in the sky to the mortals on the earth. The verse refers to the word, which is the essence of language. So, the word emerges *before* language in the poem. I claim that this indicates that we are moving toward the pre-linguistic level.

The imagery of sowing and seed, of cultivation and germination, in the second verse can be related to Heidegger's characterizations elsewhere of the word as the primordial harvest and foregathering of beyng.[27] The imagery can also be associated with his interpretation of a verse from Hölderlin's poem "Germania": "Language is the flower of the mouth. In language the earth blossoms toward the bloom of the sky."[28] What transpires before language blossoms unfolds in silence; a silence, which I maintain corresponds with the primordial silencing of the word (as discussed in section 7.1).

The third verse depicts the depth as the site from which the seed of the word is brought to ripeness in the saying. The depth is the earth. The right time for the harvesting is when the seed ripens. Its ripening time culminates in the saying. Such saying emerges on the earth. So, I identify it as the saying of the mortals. It springs from the saying of the word, which is not that of the mortals, but of beyng. In the section before the poem, Heidegger refers to the word as "the brightening secret" (*der heiternde Hehl*). The word brightens in that it "illuminates gladdening while it indicates-points to (*be-deutet*) the jointure of beyng." To "indicate-point" here means "to go on in *hints* and to conduct into the secret."[29] Thus, the word says in that it discloses at the same time that it conceals. The saying of the word is always a soundless showing. In my interpretation, the saying of mortals in this verse is also soundless, for language has yet to be born. In this sense, we have not yet left the pre-linguistic level.

The fourth verse refers to the silence and what is unspoken. Both are on the scene before language. In the verse's depiction, the silence guards or watches over (*hütet*), preserving, and protecting what is unspoken, that is, leaving it unspoken. What is unspoken is what does not show itself in speech, in word-sounds, in language. In other sections of the manuscript, Heidegger says,

"Unspoken is the word. Unspoken is language too" and "The saying is what is *unspoken.*" Here, silence guards the word, the saying, and language as such. Guarding what does not show itself in speech is not mere "non-expression," for something may be expressed in word-sounds and still remain unshown.[30] In this manner, what is unspoken remains unshown in a silence that is more original than language, which has yet to be born in the poem. Thus, I would argue that the verse refers to the primordial silence at the pre-linguistic level of determination.

Language seems to be born in the fifth verse. The verse identifies it as the home of the human being and depicts this home as something that is built. Heidegger elsewhere resorts to the images of house and home to define language as the sheltering medium of being that defines the mortals as the sonorous sayers, as those who show in word-sounds.[31] What is unusual now is that the poem appears to depict the *emergence* of this home as a birth. Yet, my sense is that this depiction fits well with the human, who is also born in this birth. It is in the home of language that the mortals are able to disclose in words their finitude and their death as death. Heidegger speaks poetically of the birth in terms of the verb "*bauen*" (to build), which means to gather, to bear, to gesture, and to gestate.[32] The poem does not say *what* builds, just as it does not say *what* sows the seed and brings it to ripeness. Is it the word that builds the home? The "it" (*ihm*) from which the pure home is built is also elusive. Is it from the silence that the home is built? I would speculate in any case that we are again at the proto-linguistic level, for the verse alludes to the emergence of language as the home of the human being, and this refers to the essence of language in relation to the essence of human being.

The sixth, seventh, and eighth verses form one sentence: "*Ehe denn der Mensch waltet sein Wesen, / Ruft zur Geburt die reine Behausung, / Ahnend die Wiege des Wohnens.*"[33] The human being and the home appear again, but in a different light. The sixth verse refers to an "ere" or a moment "before" (*Ehe denn*) humans rule their essence. In my reading, the image of humans commanding or ruling their essence refers to the modern technological rule of en-framing, that is, to what Heidegger elsewhere characterizes as *Ge-stell.* In the manuscript, he associates "the inhuman in the human being" with "*technē* and the forging ahead of beings before being" and with the human's "*failure before the word.*"[34] So, my contention is that the verse points to what would take place *before* we reach the modern technological supremacy of the inhuman: the call.

The calling announced in the seventh verse is an address, an appeal, an invocation that is silent. It calls to birth and thus invokes the pure home. This is the only time that the word "*Geburt*" (birth) appears in the poem. In my interpretation, the pure home represents language as the word of beyng in the appropriating-event. The call moves *from* and *back to* the pure home. In this sense, I claim that the poem itself is also a call *for* a rebirth, a transformation of humans in relation to their home, to language.[35] The poem is silent in this call and in its silence seeks to be in co-respondence with the primordial call.

In the final verse, the primordial call presages the cradle (*Wiege*) of the dwelling. While the image of the cradle is unusual in Heidegger, I would argue that it fits with the poetic imagery of birth. In the manuscript, he refers to it as the "cradle of beyng" (*Wiege des Seyns*).[36] He also refers to the "cradling womb" of the event in which "the human essence is sown as its remembrance [*Gedächtnis*]."[37] Perhaps in the same vein, he refers to "the twofold" of the height and the depth, which he associates with "the twofold of the human essence."[38] In a manner suggestive of heterosexual gender roles and reproduction, he relates height and depth to the sole insistent man and the sole insistent woman, respectively. In my reading, all these images convey the idea that our essence as the sonorous sayers is defined, supported, and borne by what he elsewhere calls the cradle or "balance of being."[39] The poem thus sings of the cradle, where the mortals dwell on the earth.[40]

In the reflections that contextualize the poem, Heidegger identifies "the Same" ("the sole One" unifying all in the appropriating-event) as "the secret" and "the riddle of the riddle." The cradle itself is secret and its making-secret (*hehlen*) is the concealing that appropriates and safeguards the mystery. It is in the same cradle of beyng that the mystery of language and the riddle of life "rest simply apart."[41] As the manuscript's subtitle suggests, Heidegger offers "a project of a presaging," and in the manuscript itself, he sketches out an intricate path toward the secret cradle of the dwelling. To learn to dwell on the earth, humans must be called in their essence. This call emerges from "the realm of the calling stillness."[42] The word is the "calling" and "hinting" stillness that silently appeals to ("calling-back") humans into their essence as the sonorous sayers.[43] The human essence is itself born in the language that is born in the event. The word silently calls humans back to language, which Heidegger identifies in the manuscript as "the dwelling place of the human essence."[44] I maintain that the event in which humans are appropriated to their essence is silent and this is the primeval silence of the stillness, which takes form in the concealing of beyng itself in its unconcealedness.

It is because humans live in the forgottenness of beyng that they have to learn how to hearken and co-respond to language in their sonorous showing. It is also because of the forgottenness that remembrance of the event is the only way that humans can learn. Following what Heidegger says elsewhere, remembrance is the gathering of thought, the thinking that recollects, recalls, and gives thanks for the gift of the "there is/it gives" (*es gibt*) of beyng.[45] As he suggests here, remembrance is granted when thinking is appropriated in the appropriating-event, which is ultimately the event of the truth of beyng, of its unconcealedness.[46]

I claim that the stillness, which here plays the role of teacher, is the silence of beyng in its concealedness, the primeval silence that is the stillness (mentioned in section 7.1). What the stillness teaches us is closely linked to remembrance. It teaches us to celebrate, and this means to commemorate. The presence of the grace, which we can associate with the bestowal of beyng in its unconcealedness, is commemorated. Beyng grants language to humans so that they can give thanks, by putting into word-sounds what it silently gives. However, the fitting commemoration is one that hearkens and co-responds in its answer to the silence of beyng, to the stillness. Heidegger refers to the stillness as "*the fore-word.*"[47] The "answering-word" (*Ant-wort*) responds to the stillness in the manner of thanking and it is sigetic in the silencing of what is unspoken. In Heidegger's terms: "The silence as thanking—Thinking and poetizing."[48]

What is unspoken, Heidegger also tells us, "is not consequence and result of silence, but instead the legacy [*Vermächtnis*] (overcoming and destiny) of the stillness."[49] Silence conceals and guards the legacy of the stillness. I maintain that we can interpret this legacy as what the stillness bequeaths, as what has its birthright, inheritance, and origin in the unconcealedness of beyng. The legacy of the stillness is a matter of destiny (*Geschick*), which we can associate with the gathering-sending (*Ge-schick*) of beyng in its unconcealedness. The legacy is a matter of "overcoming" or "distortion" (*Verwindung*). Overcoming thus involves a dis-tortion or twisting out of the concealedness of beyng. It is through this twisting out of the primordial silence that language can eventually burst forth in its sonorousness. In Heidegger's quasi-poetic description: "*Language tears away* / the word—from the stillness. / Removing from the rift and bearing forth in the sounding and the voice."[50]

In my reading, language (the sonorous showing) tears *away* the word (the silent showing) *from* the stillness (the deepest silence). However, I would like to emphasize that this does not mean that "the sounding" (*das Lauten*) and the voice break the stillness itself in their sonorousness. Heidegger suggests quasi-poetically that the stillness "stills" (*stillt*) and in its stilling, it is, "Concealing / Connected everywhere to the word, though not yet breaking, / but instead hinting."[51] Thus, the stillness silently teaches humans to commemorate the secret of beyng and the mystery of language so that they may learn to dwell on the earth.

In conclusion, it is fitting that the poem does not name, but instead silently shows the stillness. At the same time, the stillness is named in the thinking and poetic words that frame the poem. In both poetry and thinking, there are various ways of sigetic saying, as Heidegger's reticent, elusive, and secretive words illustrate. Hearkening is required in the co-respondence to the silence of beyng. All sigetic ways, including those that hearken by refraining from speaking and naming, are ways of saying, and this means of showing. Sigetic showing is at the same time a concealing that aims to "echo" the concealedness of beyng itself.[52]

In his different sigetic showings of the stillness throughout the manuscript, Heidegger poses questions to himself concerning the stillness, for example, by asking: "But what is *stilling*? (What does it still?)."[53] He also insists overall on the need for "carefulness in speech" and the "slowness of the path" of the "heaviest thinking."[54] It is worth noting that, in contrast with the stillness, "what is unspoken" is named in both poem and reflections. However, Heidegger also asks, "Why is now—in the descent—the saying of what is unspoken necessary for the preparation of language from the word?" Highlighting the danger posed in saying what is unspoken, he appears to emphasize here the need for that saying to be sigetic, as the "*descent in concealed language*," which appropriates only what is "concealed" in a "more original ascent," and where "[what] is residual ends only in devastation."[55]

My sense is that the notions of ascent and descent could relate to the arising and submerging movement characterizing the unconcealedness of beyng. They could also relate to the height and depth that measure the abiding expanse in the birth of language. We could then infer that what is residual is what is unconcealed and that the devastation refers to the oblivion of beyng in the modern technological age. The saying that follows the path of ascent to what is concealed and the descent in concealed language would thus be sigetic in its preservation of what is concealed.

As we will see in the next chapter, in the works that Heidegger later makes public, he names and speaks of language, the word, silence, and the stillness in ways that are reminiscent of his earlier poem and reflections. Presumably, he felt the time was ripe for responding to the need of beyng for the sonorous saying. Thus, he began to disclose what he formerly withheld. However, these disclosures on his part are selective with regard to the earlier formulations. One can conjecture that he later deemed some of the ideas and images inadequate for various reasons, in particular, for their metaphysical connotations. All the same, his later words continue to take an elusive and reticent form. Perhaps, some are still encrypted as well.

NOTES

1. Cf. Martin Heidegger, *Zum Wesen der Sprache und Zur Frage nach der Kunst* (Frankfurt am Main: Klostermann, 2010) / GA 74, 20, 122, 132, 135, 152. "*Verschweigung*" is translated as "requiescence" in Heidegger, *Heraclitus. The Inception of Occidental Thinking and Logic: Heraclitus's Doctrine of the* Logos, trans. Julia Goesser Assaiante and S. Montgomery Ewegen (London: Bloomsbury Academic, 2018). See chapter 6 for my discussion of this work.

2. Heidegger, GA74, 152. "*Das Schweigen*" is translated as "quiesence" in Heidegger, *Heraclitus. The Inception of Occidental Thinking and Logic: Heraclitus's Doctrine of the* Logos, ibid. A similar characterization of silence as "the incapacity to say" and as "renunciation of speech" is found in Heidegger, *The Event*, trans. Richard Rojcewicz (Bloomington and Indianapolis: Indiana University Press, 2013), 267 / GA71, 308.

3. Ibid. "*Erschweigen*" is translated as "acquieting" in Heidegger, *Heraclitus. The Inception of Occidental Thinking and Logic: Heraclitus's Doctrine of the* Logos.

4. In *The Event*, Heidegger identifies two forms of silence that would fit with his idea of silencing here: silence "as *expectation and unfolding* of a long preparation, without regard to oneself and not determined by ability and inability" and "as *being greeted*, which is a silence that does not exclude speech, but also does not allow just any speech. Instead, it requires a particular word of inceptual necessity" (268 / GA71, 308).

5. Heidegger, GA74, 152.

6. Ibid., 29.

7. Ibid., 132.

8. Ibid., 152.

9. Cf. ibid., 59, 132.

10. Ibid., 152.

11. Ibid., 132.

12. Ibid., 62.

13. Ibid., 87.

14. Ibid., 150.

15. Ibid., 62–63. Cf. ibid., 132. In *The Event*, Heidegger says, "What inceptually disposes (*stimmt*) is the still-soundless voice (*Stimme*) of the word." Accordingly, in this attuning or disposing voice that is the word, there is "neither speaking out nor silence," and it "knows neither utterance nor silence and stillness" (145–46 / GA71, 171–72).

16. In *The Event*, Heidegger characterizes this fullness in terms of the "treasure of the word" and describes the word as "the ground of the subsequent formation of 'word meanings' and 'word sounds,'" which "arise concurrently and arise every time the word-sound is intoned" (145 / GA71, 170–71).

17. Heidegger, GA74, 18–19.

18. Ibid., 50–54.

19. Ibid., 152.

20. Cf. ibid., 58–59, 153–54.

21. Ibid., 19.

22. The 1944 Heraclitus summer seminar is referenced in the manuscript and the editor notes that Heidegger presented it as a birthday gift to a friend in 1945 (Heidegger, GA74, 208). Because of copyright and translation restrictions, I cannot quote or translate the entire poem.

23. Heidegger, *Contributions to Philosophy (Of the Event),* trans. Richard Rojcewicz and Daniela Vallega-Neu (Bloomington and Indianapolis: Indiana University Press, 2012), 95 / 79.

24. Heidegger, GA74, 53.

25. Heidegger discusses "earth" and "world" in prose elsewhere (GA74, 43). Cf. Heidegger, "The Nature of Language," in *On the Way to Language*, 100 / US, 207.

26. Heidegger, GA74, 43–44. Cf. "Language," in Martin Heidegger, *Poetry, Language, Thought*, trans. Albert Hofstadter (New York, Harper & Row, 1971), 199 / US, 21.

27. Heidegger interprets the original sense of *legein* in terms of harvesting and gathering as well. For an example from the same period, see: Heidegger, *Heraclitus. The Inception of Occidental Thinking and Logic: Heraclitus's Doctrine of the Logos*, §5 / GA55. See also chapter 6 for my discussion of this term. For a later example, see Heidegger, "Words," in *On the Way to Language*, 155 / US, 237.

28. Heidegger, "The Nature of Language," 99 / US, 206.

29. Heidegger, GA74, 43.

30. Heidegger, GA74, 60–62. Heidegger twice references his 1934–35 interpretation of the verse in Hölderlin's poem "Germania," which refers to what is unspoken. There, he identifies language as what is unspoken in the dialogue between Zeus's eagle and the quietest daughter of God. See: Heidegger, *Hölderlin's Hymns "Germania" and "The Rhein,"* trans. William McNeill and Julia Anne Ireland (Indiana: Indiana University Press, 2014) / GA39. For a later reference to what is unspoken, see Heidegger, "The Way to Language," 122 / US, 253.

31. See, for example, Heidegger, "Letter on Humanism" in *Pathmarks*, ed. William McNeill (Cambridge: Cambridge University Press, 1998) / GA9. See also Heidegger, "The Way to Language," 129 / US, 260; and "Language," 209–10 / US, 31–33.

32. Heidegger, "Building Dwelling Thinking," in *Poetry, Language, Thought*, 146–51 / VA, 148–53.

33. Ibid., 43, 49.

34. Ibid., 63.

35. See: Heidegger, "The Way to Language," where Heidegger talks about "a transformation of language" (135 / US, 267).

36. Heidegger, GA74, 51–52. Heidegger plays on the relation between the German words for cradle and balance (*Wiege*), bearing weight (*Wiegen*), weighing (*Wägen*), scales and wager *(Wage)*, way (*Weg*) and way-making or moving-waying (*Be-wegen*). Cf. Heidegger, "What are Poets For?," in *Poetry, Language, Thought*, 103–104 / GA5, 280–81.

37. Ibid., 47.

38. Ibid., 49.

39. Heidegger, "What Are Poets For?," 104 / GA5, 281.

40. Cf. Heidegger, "Building Dwelling Thinking," 150 / VA, 152; "Language," 200 / US, 22.

41. Heidegger, GA74, 43–44, 51.

42. Ibid., 50–51.

43. Ibid., 46–49.

44. Ibid., 58.

45. Heidegger, *What Is Called Thinking?*, trans. J. Glenn Gray (New York: Harper and Row), 1968 / GA8. Cf. Heidegger, "The Nature of Language," 88 / US, 194.
46. Heidegger, GA74, 61–62.
47. Ibid., 59.
48. Ibid., 63.
49. Ibid., 61.
50. Ibid., 58–59.
51. Ibid. For a later depiction of the "stilling" of stillness, see Heidegger, "Language," 205–06 / US, 27–28.
52. Ibid., 61–62.
53. Ibid., 58.
54. Ibid., 52–53.
55. Ibid., 58.

Chapter 8

The Soundless Peal of the Stillness

This chapter concludes the chronology of Heidegger's thoughts on silence. *On the Way to Language* represents a culminating stage in which he makes public a distilled version of the earlier quiet musings and reticent sayings that we have examined in chapter 7. I claim that the idea of the "peal of the stillness" epitomizes the distillation of his meditations on the relation between silence, language, and truth. However, while in the earlier manuscript the truth of beyng in the appropriating-event provides the explicit framework for the inquiry into the essence of language, we find no explicit references to "truth" as he ponders the relations between language and silence. My sense is that its workings can be inferred from what Heidegger says and suggests.

In two of the six essays of the collection, Heidegger focuses expressly on *Ereignis*, rather than on being/beyng, in his pursuit of the way to language.[1] We find an explanation for this change of accent in one of those essays. He claims there that we need to reflect on the appropriating-event as such, which is "richer" than being in its definition, though being can be thought in terms of the event of appropriation when we reflect on its "essential origin."[2] More categorically, Heidegger states that the appropriating-event is "the giving-yield (*Er-gebnis*) that gives (*gibt*) a 'there is' (*es gibt*) . . . of which even Being itself stands in need to come into its own presence."[3] In this light, Heidegger focuses explicitly on the appropriating (*das Ereignen*) and owning (*das Eignen*) of the appropriating-event, in and through which the unconcealedness of beyng unfolds. I maintain, then, that the truth of beyng is at work in these dynamics of *Ereignis*.

I also claim that Heidegger's characterization of the essence of language as the saying that shows hints at an original unconcealedness as well. We find one of his more perspicuous enunciations of this definition in one of the essays: "Showing . . . causes to appear what is present and to fade from appearance what is absent . . . all radiant appearance and all fading away is grounded in the showing Saying."[4] In my reading, what is present and what is absent *precede* their showing. In his interpretation of Aristotle's notion of *semeia* as "that which shows," Heidegger is more explicit in basing showing on unconcealment as he explains that it means "showing, in the sense of bringing about the appearance, which in its turn consists in the prevalence of unconcealment (*alētheia*)."[5] Focusing on his own notion of showing, he alludes to that prevalence by emphasizing that "[s]elf-showing appearance is the mark of the presence and the absence of everything that is present," so that all showing is "preceded by an indication" from what shows itself "that it will let itself be shown."[6] Inspired by the poets Trakl and Pindar, whose poems sing of the "splendor of gold," Heidegger also suggests that the speaking of language as the bidding of world and things to come to presence "keeps and holds everything present in the unconcealedness of its appearing."[7] Thus, I claim that all this indicates the primacy of unconcealedness, as the presencing and absencing of beyng itself, in relation to showing. In this light, we can see that it is only on the abyssal-ground of the truth of beyng that showing "lets beings appear in their '*it is*.'"[8]

In my reading, the owning and the appropriating of the appropriating-event unfold in and through the essence of language as the saying that shows. In this vein, Heidegger claims: "Saying, the nature of language is the appropriating showing."[9] In the same vein, he emphasizes: "*The moving force in Showing of Saying is Owning*." This owning takes the form of showing, which presupposes the manifestness of beings: "It is what brings all present and absent beings each into their own, from where they show themselves in what they are, and where they abide according to their kind."[10] Accordingly, even the guide-word "the language of being" points to owning, insofar as it means that "language belongs to this persisting being, is proper to [*eignet*] what moves all things because that is its most distinctive property [*als dessen Eigenstes*]."[11]

I maintain that the three main forms of silence that Heidegger had considered in his earlier manuscripts (the human hearkening and reticent co-respondence, the primordial silencing of the word, and the stillness to which the primeval silence of beyng belongs) reappear throughout the essay collection. Where he focuses expressly on *Ereignis*, they are defined in terms of the appropriating-event that appropriates (*ereignet*) mortals to co-respond and makes them appropriate (*vereignet*) to saying as showing. They also reappear in the essays that take another course on the way to language through its essential definition as the saying that shows. In what follows, I will identify each form of silence as it appears in these different contexts, while I highlight their respective links to truth as the unconcealedness of beyng.

Beginning with the deepest form of silence that belongs to the stillness itself, it is worth emphasizing that it must be distinguished from its peal insofar as the stillness *precedes* the peal as such. More specifically, it is as language in its essence or as saying that shows that the stillness peals. My point is that we are at the pre-linguistic level with the peal. The soundless peal is not the primeval silence that belongs to the stillness, but instead the primordial silencing of the word. It is *language* in its essence that silently speaks, it is the silent *saying* that appropriates and shows, it is the soundless gathering that *calls—as* the peal of the stillness. Such speaking, saying, and calling can arise only in the breaking, in the rending of the stillness in its peal. I claim, then, that the stillness is the site of the original concealedness of beyng (at the proto-linguistic level), and its peal is the *un*concealedness that unfolds (at the pre-linguistic level) in the appropriating-event.

In his interpretation of Georg Trakl's poem "A Winter Evening," Heidegger recasts the first line of the second stanza, "Wandering ones, more than a few" as those "mortals who wander on dark courses" and "who are capable of dying." In death, he says, "the supreme concealedness of being crystallizes," or rather, gathers itself (*versammelt sich*).[12] In this light, I would add that it is in the stillness that the supreme concealedness of beyng rests. "To rest," means not only to be still, to stay, but also to be silent— in the musical sense of a pause or an interval of silence. The stillness stills beyng in its concealedness and is thus the supreme silence and the supreme rest. As Heidegger tells us, the stillness itself

> is in no way merely the soundless. In soundlessness there persists merely the lack of the motion of entoning, sounding. But the motionless is neither limited to sounding by being its suspension, nor is it itself already something genuinely tranquil. The motionless itself still rests on rest. As the stilling of stillness, rest, conceived strictly, is always more in motion than all motion and always more restlessly active than any agitation.[13]

Heidegger advises us that authentic hearing in its self-restraint "must take care not just to hear the peal of the stillness afterward, but to *hear it even beforehand* [vor-zu-hören], and thus as it were to anticipate its command."[14] I maintain that this anticipatory hearing of the peal suggests a deeper form of hearkening that reaches ahead to the very onset of the breaking of the stillness. This point would be the inceptual moment (*Augenblick*), the blink of the eye (*Augen-blick*), of the *un*concealedness of beyng in the appropriating-event, in which beyng flashes away, as it were, into its concealedness in the stillness. Heidegger suggests as much in his depiction of the appropriation of the hearkening mortals for the sonorous saying as a beholding (*Er-äugen*) of their human essence for the saying of what avows (zu-*sagt*) itself to them in the saying of that which is everywhere concealed.[15]

However, the most insistent hearkening toward the supreme silence of the stillness and the most peering moment of the blink of the eye toward the concealedness of beyng are extreme possibilities for the mortals who must await in anticipation to hear/submit to/obey the command of the appropriating-event. I claim that Heidegger correspondingly leaves open the questions that teeter on the brink of the stillness, as the following example shows: "On what does the stillness break? How does the broken stillness shape the mortal speech that sounds in verses and sentences?"[16]

At the same time, I maintain that, in his reticence concerning the stillness, Heidegger manages to hint at the tentative answers hidden in these questions. In this manner, he proffers intimations, not only about the stilling of stillness but also about its breaking and its occurrence as the movement of being face-to-face with one another (*Gegen-ein-ander-über*), within the fourfold.[17] He also intimates its relation to saying, as its "stream," and to the undiscussed region of the origin of showing.[18] Moreover, he is able to stretch these indications—indirectly—through and beyond his characterizations of the peal of the stillness, for it is ultimately *the stillness* that peals. Furthermore, the stillness continues its stilling in and through the peal.

In my interpretation, the *dis*closive power of language in its essence as the appropriative speaking, saying, showing, letting-appear, clearing, and calling—in sum, as the peal of the stillness, stems from the stillness, just as *un*concealedness stems from the original concealedness in the appropriating-event. The silencing and soundlessness that characterize the essence of language in its disclosive role hark back to the supreme silence that pertains to the stillness, to the primeval silence of beyng. In this harking back to the original concealedness, language in its essence itself resonates forth at the same time as a concealing. Heidegger thus characterizes saying as "the lighting-*concealing*-releasing offer of world" that "holds and keeps" the world's regions in that "*it holds itself . . . in reserve*."[19] In the same vein, he suggests that saying is self-concealing insofar as the essence of language is "the appropriating showing which *disregards precisely itself*, in order to free that which it shows to its authentic appearance."[20] The self-concealing of the word is also intimated in that it has a "*hidden* essence (verbal) which *invisibly* in its Saying and even already in what is unsaid, extends to us the thing as a thing."[21] More specifically, the word is self-concealing as "mystery" and as such "remains remote," so that "there is no word for it . . . no Saying which could bring the being of language to language."[22] Heidegger issues a similar claim concerning the self-concealing of the being of language, and he thereby hints at the stillness as its essential origin and at the withdrawal of beyng into concealedness: "Thus language not only holds back when we speak it in accustomed ways, but this holding back is determined by the fact that language *holds back its origin* and so *denies its being* to our usual notions."[23] The original concealedness is also reflected in the fact that saying and being "belong to each other in a veiled way."[24]

I maintain that throughout the different essays of the collection, Heidegger configures the primordial silencing of the word within complex structures of disclosure that take form in and through the unconcealedness of beyng in the appropriating-event. However, even when he focuses explicitly on *Ereignis*, these structures are configured differently: in the earliest essay of the collection (1950), "Language," the prevailing structures are the fourfold of the world and the dif-ference of world and thing, whereas in the latest essay (1959), "The Way to Language," they are the rending design (*Auf-riß*) of the unifying unity of the being of language and the way-making (*Be-wegen*) of language through which the appropriating-event grants to mortals their abode. Other essays repeat or introduce structures and dynamics of disclosure, for example: "The Nature of Language" refers to language as the saying of the unitary fourfold of the world and to saying as the world-moving (*Welt-bewëgendes*) relation of all relations. Language, as the saying that shows, is the relation of human essence to the twofold (being/beings) of unconcealedness in "A Dialogue on Language."[25] I claim that all these structures are compatible with one another insofar as they can be said to highlight different aspects of the disclosive power of language in its essence.

I claim that all the structures of disclosure are soundless as well. Their soundlessness ultimately is derived from the stillness, even as it breaks and rends in the appropriating-event of the unconcealedness of beyng. Some of the structures reflect the supreme tension of the unconcealedness—the wresting away from the original concealedness and the withdrawal back into concealedness. This reflection can be perceived more readily in the twofold (being/beings), in the en-counter (*Ent-gegnung*) of the four world-regions, in the rending design of language, the strife of earth and world, and in the dif-ference of world and thing. The dynamism of the unfolding of truth in the appropriating-event may also be discerned in its replication in the way-making and world-moving that language enacts.

I believe that it is significant that Heidegger explicitly refers to the stillness as what "takes place [*ereignet sich*]" in "the double stilling of the dif-ference" of world and thing.[26] In my interpretation, this reference reveals how the stillness extends itself to what is disclosed in the saying that shows. The same extension can be seen in the time and space of the fourfold, which "rests in stillness," or rather, rests still (*ruht still*). Heidegger also indicates that the timing of time and the spacing of space, or time's "removing and bringing to us" and space's "throwing open, admitting and releasing," both "belong together in the Same, the play of stillness." It is worth noting that he declines to talk about this play; it is "something to which we cannot here give further thought."[27] While this decision may not be entirely driven by the principle of reticence, my sense is that it does signal the fact that another sort of reflection is necessary, namely, the thinking of the *essence* of stillness, which stills in and through the soundless saying that shows.

Heidegger repeatedly refers to the "need" of language in its essence as the soundless saying for the sonorous saying of the mortals.[28] As these claims suggest, neither the need, nor the soundlessness of the primordial saying indicate a lack or an absence; instead, they point to the appropriating-event in which beyng in its truth gives itself at the same time that it withdraws. It is in and through this appropriation that humans are freed to their proper essence as the sonorous sayers.

The resounding of language in the speech of the mortals is not something like a supplement to or an enhancement of the soundless saying; rather, resounding is the reverberation in word-sounds that it enables in its disclosive showing and calling. In this vein, Heidegger proposes that our reflection "must be guided by the hidden riches that language holds in store for us, so that these riches may summon us to the saying of language."[29] It is from these hidden riches that "we demand, reach out and call for the sound that is already kept in store for us."[30] I maintain that both the need and the wealth stem ultimately from the stillness, insofar as the soundlessness of saying and the hiddenness of language in its essence derive from the primeval silence, from the supreme concealedness of beyng itself.

The peal of the stillness rings for humans and for the sake of humans, bidding them to their own essence as the mortals—the sonorous sayers that are appropriated in the soundless saying or speaking of language in its essence. Thus, Heidegger claims that "only as" humans "belong within the peal of the stillness are mortals able to speak in *their own* way in sounds."[31] In his depiction, the "sound" of language emerges in its "earthyness" through the "sounding of the voice" of the mortals who dwell upon the earth. Emphasizing the primordial disclosedness that unfolds in the peal of the stillness, he indicates that it is from the soundless saying, "in which it comes to pass that World is made to appear." The "sound of speaking" has "its source" in this saying and is accordingly "held with the harmony that attunes the regions of the world-structure, playing them in chorus."[32] The choral play of the fourfold is soundless and its soundlessness derives from the supreme silence of beyng. In the same vein, the harmony that attunes the world-regions and thus discloses them in their unity can only arise from the supreme tension of the unconcealedness. Once again, I claim that the ultimate source of all saying—the soundless as well as the resounding—is the stillness from which beyng in its truth breaks through and toward which beyng retreats.

The silence of the mortals of the fourfold takes two forms in relation to the peal of the stillness, namely, as a listening and as a co-responding to the peal. Both forms require that humans hold themselves in openness and hold themselves back in reserve. In this manner, humans are in a fundamental attunement with the disclosive and silent saying, which as clearing opens and holds the openness at the same time that it holds itself back in reserve. In this sense, Heidegger claims that we hear the soundless saying, "only because we belong within it."[33] To listen to language is thus to "*let* it say its Saying to us," to "*let* its soundless voice come to us," *receiving* what it shows to us in its disclosive essence.[34] Heidegger grounds the human ability to speak in this fundamental listening. It is the soundless saying itself that commands us to be silent in our listening and our saying, for it "demands of us that we achieve by silence the appropriating initiating movement within the being of language—and do so without talking about silence."[35]

However, Heidegger also refers to the special way of listening to language, which he labels "authentic" and which I believe can be distinguished as the hearkening that is possible only in thinking and poetry. Thus, for example, the model of an "authentic gesture of thinking" involves "listening to the grant" of being in saying.[36] Listening to "the unspoken" by language as the soundless saying also distinguishes the authentic form of thinking.[37] The same applies to the "saying-after" (*nach-sagen*) in the poet's work, which for "the longest time—before . . . spoken, is . . . only a listening."[38] This reflects the fact that poetry and thinking have a "distinctive, though in each case different, relation to language, [that] is proper to them both."[39] Thus, Heidegger claims, "the being of language, as Saying that shows, rests on Appropriation which makes us humans over to the releasement in which we can listen freely, therefore the way-making of Saying into speech first opens up for us the paths along which our thinking can pursue the *authentic* way to language."[40] With regard to the hearkening in poetry and thinking, what is distinctive is that it attends to the saying in its clearing and concealing *as such*. The other form of listening, which defines the human ability to speak, attends to *what* the saying shows. My contention is that both forms of listening attend to the soundless saying, but only poetry and thinking are attuned to its showing and its soundlessness, and they are thus able to hearken to the peal of the stillness.

Heidegger constantly depicts all mortal speech as a sonorous co-responding that is appropriated by language in its essence, as the primordial saying that shows and as the peal of the stillness.[41] However, there are different ways of co-responding. Everything that is "spoken stems in a variety of ways from the unspoken," so "what is spoken remains many-sided."[42] All "mortals heed the bidding call of the stillness of the dif-ference," but this happens "even when they do not know that call." Presumably, those mortals who *do* know the call here, co-respond in a "speaking that listens and accepts," and this response is a "receptive listening" that is "at the same time a recognition that makes due acknowledgment.[43]

I believe it is evident that poetry and thinking as the distinctive forms of listening to what is unspoken are also distinctive ways of co-responding. Heidegger identifies "anticipation in reserve" as "what genuinely belongs to responding."[44] Those who attend to the "message of the two-fold's unconcealment" are those who walk "the boundary of the boundless" and "seek the boundary's mystery."[45] The thinker adopts the "[q]uiet consideration" that "makes possible the insight into how nearness and Saying . . . are the Same."[46] The poet remains quiet as well through the poem, which "shelters" what is its spoken as that which is essentially "unspoken."[47] Poets and thinkers respond to the deepest silences in what Heidegger calls an "essential Saying," which "hearkens back to [the] veiled mutual belonging of Saying and Being." Thus, he explicitly characterizes both poetry and thinking here as a "distinctive Saying in that they remain delivered over to the mystery of the word."[48] The sayings of poets and thinkers are silent in their attunement to the silent peal of the stillness: "Silence corresponds to the soundless tolling of the stillness of appropriating-showing-Saying."[49] The reticence and reserve of poets and thinkers in their responding is thus appropriated by the peal of the stillness: "Every authentic hearing holds back with its own saying. For hearing keeps to itself in the listening by which it remains appropriated to the peal of the stillness. All responding is attuned to this restraint that reserves itself."[50]

The following figure summarizes in outline format the complex relations between silence, language, and truth (in terms of appropriating-event) that I have uncovered in Heidegger's later thinking of the peal of stillness:

(A) Human silence: Mortal hearkening and reticent co-responding

- Resounding: Sonorous saying/showing
- Uncovering and covering
- Mortals appropriated and made appropriate

(1) Linguistic level

(B) Primordial silence: The peal/the ringing

- Soundless saying/showing/clearing of the word (and its disclosive structures):
    - En-counter of the four world-regions
    - Rending-design of language
    - Twofold of being/beings
    - Strife of world/earth
    - Dif-ference of world/thing
    - Way-making/World-moving
- Self-concealing unconcealment
- Appropriating and owning the mortals

(2) Pre-linguistic level

(C) Primeval silence: The stillness

- Soundless stilling
- Original concealment and supreme rest
- Appropriation

(3) Proto-linguistic level

The Appropriating-event

Figure 8.1

In conclusion, in his role as the thinker of the peal of the stillness, Heidegger's own saying remains most reticent about the stillness itself in the essays of the collection because he thereby tries to co-respond to the primeval silence. At the same time, he is increasingly more vocal about the danger that the language of framing or en-framing conceals in itself.[51] Given that "language always speaks according to the mode in which the Appropriation as such reveals itself or withdraws," the most pressing task for thinking is to inquire into the appropriating-event of the truth of beyng.[52] Thus, I maintain that Heidegger's inquiry quietly continues to draw from the concept of the stillness as he repeatedly sounds the warning on the dangers that challenge-forth in the noisy and frenzied age of the "language-machine."[53]

NOTES

1. Martin Heidegger, *On the Way to Language*, trans. Peter D. Hertz (New York: Harper & Row, 1971) / US. The two essays in which Heidegger focuses on *Ereignis* in his reflections on language are "Language" and "The Way to Language."
2. Heidegger, "The Way to Language," in *On the Way to Language*, 129 / US, 260 (footnote).
3. Ibid., 127 / US, 258.
4. Ibid., 126 / US, 257.
5. Ibid., 115 / US, 245.
6. Ibid., 123 / US, 254.
7. Heidegger, "Language," 201 / US, 23.
8. Heidegger, "Words," in *On the Way to Language*, 155 / US, 237.
9. Heidegger, "The Way to Language," 131 / US, 262.
10. Ibid., 127 / US, 258.
11. Heidegger, "The Nature of Language," in *On the Way to Language*, 95 / US, 201.
12. Heidegger, "Language," 200 / US, 22.
13. Ibid., 206–07 / US, 28–29.
14. Ibid., 209 / US, 31. Emphasis added.
15. Heidegger, "The Way to Language," 129 / US, 260.
16. Heidegger, "Language," 208 / US, 30. Cf. Heidegger, "The Nature of Language," 106 / US 214; and "The Way to Language," 124–26 / US 255–58.
17. Heidegger, "The Essence of Language," 107–08 / US, 214–16.
18. Heidegger, "The Way to Language," 124–25 / US, 255.
19. Heidegger, "The Nature of Language," 107 / US, 215. Emphases added. Cf. ibid., 93 / US, 200.
20. Heidegger, "The Way to Language," 131 / US, 262. Emphasis added.

21. Heidegger, "Words," 154 / US, 236. Emphasis added. Cf. "The Nature of Language," 91 / US, 197.

22. Ibid.

23. Heidegger, "The Nature of Language," 81 / US, 185–86. Emphases added.

24. Heidegger, "Words," 155 / US, 237.

25. Heidegger, "A Dialogue on Language," in *On the Way to Language*, 40 / US, 135.

26. Heidegger, "Language," 206 / US, 28.

27. Heidegger, "The Nature of Language," 106 / US, 214.

28. Cf. Heidegger, "Language," 208 / US, 30; "The Nature of Language," 90 / US, 196; "The Way to Language," 129 / US, 260; 134 / US, 266.

29. Heidegger, "The Nature of Language," 91 / US, 197.

30. Heidegger, "The Way to Language," 124 / US, 255.

31. Heidegger, "Language," 208 / US, 30. Cf. Heidegger, "The Way to Language": "Saying keeps the way open along which speaking, as listening, catches from Saying what is to be said, and raises what it thus has caught and received into the sounding word" (131 / US, 262).

32. Heidegger, "The Nature of Language," 101 / US, 208.

33. Heidegger, "The Way to Language," 124 / US, 255.

34. Ibid. Emphases added. Cf. Heidegger, "Language": "Mortals speak by responding to language in a twofold way, receiving and replying" (209 / US, 31).

35. Ibid., 134–35 / US, 266.

36. Heidegger, "The Nature of Language," 71–72 / US, 175. Cf. ibid., 76 / US, 180.

37. Heidegger, "The Way to Language," 131 / US, 262.

38. Heidegger, "Language in the Poem," in *On the Way to Language*, 188 / US, 70.

39. Ibid., 161 / US, 38.

40. Heidegger, "The Way to Language," 130 / US, 261. Emphasis added.

41. Cf. Heidegger, "Language," 209 / US, 31; and "The Way to Language," 129 / US, 260; 135 / US, 267.

42. Heidegger, "The Way to Language," 120 / US, 251.

43. Heidegger, "Language," 209 / US, 31. Cf. Heidegger, "A Dialogue on Language," 40 / US, 135.

44. Heidegger, "Language," 210 / US, 33.

45. Heidegger, "A Dialogue on Language," 41 / US, 137. The last sentence is said by the Japanese in response to the Inquirer.

46. Heidegger, "The Nature of Language," 107 / US, 214.

47. Heidegger, "Language in the Poem," 188 / US, 70.

48. Heidegger, "Words," 156–56 / US, 238.

49. Heidegger, "The Way to Language," 131 / US, 262.

50. Heidegger, "Language" 209 / US, 31. Taking on the guise of the thinker as the poet, Heidegger earlier (in 1947) wrote a poem about the appropriated restraint, where he suggests that such appropriation comes from the stillness. See Heidegger, "The Thinker as Poet" in *Poetry, Language, Thought*, 11 / GA13, 77.

51. Cf. Heidegger, "A Dialogue on Language," 25 / US, 116; "The Nature of Language,"102–04 / US, 209–11; "The Way to Language," 131–33 / US, 262–64.

52. Heidegger, "The Way to Language," 131 / US, 262.

53. Heidegger, "Hebel-Friend of the House" trans. B.V. Flotz and M. Heim, *Contemporary German Philosophy* 3(1983): 89–101 / HH.

Chapter 9

Sounding Out the Later Meanings of Silence

In this chapter, which is divided into three sections, I tune mostly into the later Heidegger's concept of silence and draw critical conclusions concerning its conceptual implications, contributions, and problems. Section 9.1 contains reflections on the relations of silence to speech and sound. Section 9.2 focuses on the contrast between the quiet co-respondence of poetry and thinking with the loud chatter of the everyday and the metaphysical silence of mysticism. Section 9.3 finalizes this book by probing into the definition of humans as the mortal sonorous sayers in relation to the hinting immortals, the languageless animals, and the loudness of the modern technological age. Throughout these critical explorations, I suggest different concepts of silence that aim to retain the richness and dynamism of Heidegger's without what I identify as its more problematic features.

9.1. THE HARMONIES AND DISHARMONIES OF SILENCE IN RELATION TO SPEECH AND SOUND

Heidegger's way to silence reaches its summit with *On the Way to Language,* where the three main forms of silence (human, primordial, and primeval) are epitomized in the soundless peal of the stillness that appropriates the mortals to co-respond in their sonorous saying. Silence pervades throughout the different levels (proto-linguistic, pre-linguistic, and linguistic) that determine sonorous speech or the saying in word-sounds. I first explore how silence relates to speech and sound at these points to expose some of the conundrums presented by this relationship.

The deepest layer—the primeval silence that pertains to the stillness—is the ultimate origin of the word (the essence of language), and, in this sense, it is at the level of the proto-linguistic determination. The stillness is the abyssal-ground of the originary concealedness from which the word itself can emerge in the appropriating-event. Heidegger's positive definition of the stillness (as the dynamic fullness from which the word breaks off in its rending) counters the traditional metaphysical definition of silence in negative terms (as the absence or lack of sounds and motion). That said, my contention is that it remains the case that in the supreme silence, there are no word-sounds, for the word itself has yet to arise. In fact, there are no sounds at all.

Evidently, the metaphysical acoustic-phonetical sound and its auditory perception are ruled out from the stillness in principle. However, the *non*-linguistic sounds of the fourfold of the world, for example, the creaking wagon, the crackling fire, the tones of the harp, the ringing of bells, are themselves excluded from the stillness. We are able to hear these sounds only because we can hearken to the soundless peal of the stillness, to the word. Moreover, to be able to hear non-linguistic sounds in the sense of interpreting them as such, for example, the ringing of bells *as* the ringing of bells, we must first be able to hear and speak in word-sounds. The word-sounds fit into the measure that is set by the soundless word, which is what gathers or assembles sonorous saying as a whole and thereby provides the structure for grasping and showing something as something. The as-structure of disclosure is thus essentially verbal. So, my contention is that, in Heidegger, the stillness is absolutely soundless, in the sense that it is a *total* silence.[1]

Once again, I claim that the supreme soundlessness of the stillness does not indicate a lack or an absence. Instead, this soundlessness is the primeval fullness, from which the sounding (*Lautung/Lauten*) and sound (*Laut*) originate as the breaking off or the rending of the stillness. However, I contend that it is valid to ask: What specifically is this sounding—for it is not itself sonorous? What specifically is this sound—for it is not a word-sound? In response, one could say that the essence of both sounding and sound belong to saying, which means that they are determined by the showing or the clearing that defines the word. So, they are essentially disclosive.

Following my line of reasoning, sounding could thus be construed as the essential *capacity* granted in the word for the sonorous disclosure that is enacted in speech. Sounding presupposes the clearing, so it is itself soundless. It is in language, understood as sonorous speech, that the resounding (*Verlauten*) of this soundless sounding takes place. The sound that originates as the rending of the stillness could be construed as the essential constituent to words in their sonorousness, that is, as word-*sounds*. It would not itself be a sound; it would be soundless, for it belongs to the *essence* of language, not to language as sonorous speech.

As I have already speculated, the soundlessness of the stillness is perhaps the originary site of the dif-ference between what is and what is not sonorous with regard to speech.[2] One could conjecture further that such dif-ference arises at the very moment of the rending *of* or breaking off *from* the stillness that define sounding and sound in their origination. Given that the soundless stillness itself stills throughout its rending, the sounding and the sound remain soundless. This stilling of the stillness continues onward, pervading not only the soundless essence of language but also stilling through the silent and soundless moments that are possible even within sonorous speech. Reticence, keeping silent, and hearkening are among these possibilities at the linguistic level of the stilling.

Heidegger's claim that language has its origin in silence applies first to the primeval silence that pertains to the stillness as the origin of the essence of language, at the level of the proto-linguistic determination. It applies as well to the primordial silence that pertains to the word in its soundless saying as the origin of language as the sonorous saying. In this sense, the soundless sounding and sound that emerge as the rending of the stillness are pre-linguistic, that is, they belong to the essence of language, which in turn determines language as sonorous saying. Put otherwise: The word in its soundless sounding and sound determines the resonating in word-sounds. Sonorous speech as such thus has this multilayered origin in silence. However, the primeval and primordial layers of silence are covered up in idle talk. So, the reticence, keeping silent, and hearkening that distinguish the authentic saying of thinkers and poets involve breaking away from idle talk to break through to the silent origin that is not only covered up but also (and more fundamentally) conceals itself.

Given that the human essence is essentially linguistic—in the sense of being the "there" of the sonorous saying of beyng, I contend that it is valid to ask: How can humans gain access to the pre-linguistic and proto-linguistic levels in which silence takes on its primordial and primeval forms? The event of appropriation, the peal of the stillness, the call of beyng, the saying of the word all emerge soundlessly from these seemingly unfathomable depths. The fundamental moods and the profound experiences in thinking and poetry that attune and appropriate the human being can occur only within and through what is the human's essential determination—language as sonorous speech, as saying that shows in word-sounds. The silences that characterize the moods and attunements, as well as the silencing experiences, are all relative to sonorous saying—in its interruptions, circumscriptions, limitations, and deprivations. I maintain that, in Heidegger, there can be no *immediate* access to the silences that determine our essence as the sonorous sayers. Put otherwise: The only way to silence is through sonorous speech. Even the hearkening to the deeper silences is mediated in Heidegger: To hearken is to listen in the manner of attending and submitting to what is soundless as soundless, but this attentiveness and submission are defined by the as-structure of sonorous speech. The word-sounds are the essential units of this as-structure, which operates when we speak and when we do not speak, when we are silent and when we are not silent.[3]

Heidegger's claims that the human being is needed by the event, beyng, and the word focus on the sonorousness that distinguishes human saying. What is soundless is not only needful of resounding but also addresses, calls, demands, uses, and appropriates the human essence for this resounding. The rending and breaking of the stillness itself thus unfolds in the direction of this need. As the sonorous "there" of beyng, Da-sein discloses in the manner of showing in word-sounds, and this showing preserves and shelters the clearing-concealing of beyng. Without this sonorous disclosure, beings themselves would not be as beings. Even more fundamentally, no silence would be as silence. In this sense, I contend that Heidegger effectively renders silence relative to the word-sounds that show it as silence. This relativity includes the primeval and primordial silences from which sonorous speech itself originates. Neither the stillness of beyng would be as this stillness, nor the mystery of the word would be as this mystery.

However, I am not maintaining that Heidegger flounders in a circle when he depicts silence as the origin of sonorous speech and portrays sonorous speech as the site needed for the disclosure of silence. Instead, I claim that the relation between origin and need could be interpreted as harmonious at the same time that it reflects the very tension of truth as clearing-concealing. Yet, this is what I call a "monotone" relation, in that it either subsumes what is non-linguistic under what is linguistic (in the sense of fitting it into the sonorous as-structure of speech) or excludes what is non-linguistic altogether. We have already considered the case of non-linguistic sounds, such as the crackling of the fire, which must first be "heard" as such through sonorous speech. I claim that, following Heidegger, the same primacy of the sonorous as-structure could be applied to other meaningful perceptions, for example, the dancing orange flames of the fire, the fragrant smell of the burning logs, the smoky taste of the food cooked over it, and its comforting heat. These experiences would thus have to be linguistically mediated to have any meaningfulness at all.

The thinkers and poets in their fundamental attunements and hearkening exemplify the harmony of silence and sonorous speech in their own reticent sayings. What of non-linguistic attunements to and co-respondences with silence? Would music qualify? Heidegger characterized poetry as the song of beyng and relied on other musical tropes, such as attunement and voice, to convey his thoughts. More directly, music could be viewed as a form of attunement to silence that is sonorous and incorporates silences in its pauses or rests but is not necessarily verbal because the sounds need not be word-sounds. So, one could argue that music enacts its own profound disclosures of silence and sound.[4]

Heidegger certainly allowed for other forms of truth in art, as evidenced in his analyses of the Ancient Greek temples and Van Gogh's painting of the peasant shoes, for example. He also included music in his critique of the common view of works of art in their "thingly character": "Beethoven's quartets lie in the storerooms of the publishing house like potatoes in a cellar."[5] With regard to music, he emphasized as well that *we* are the ones who hear music (a Bach fugue, in his example), not the ear.[6] However, unlike music, painting and architecture are not *intrinsically* related to silence and sound.[7] Yet, I claim that, for Heidegger, all these other ways of disclosing can unfold only within the clearing of the word as the soundless saying that needs the sonorous saying, which is first founded in the word-sounds of poets.[8] Furthermore, what distinguishes the poetic and thinking sayings as inaugural is that they endeavor to co-respond with the soundless silences of beyng and the word in the appropriating-event. So, for Heidegger, there is in effect only one authentic form of harmony between silence and the human being as the sonorous sayer.

While Heidegger took great pains to distinguish his reflections on silence, sound, and speech from the metaphysics of objective presence, he did acknowledge that he was still within the horizon of the metaphysical distinction between what is sensible and supersensible.[9] I claim that this distinction can be easily read into the tropes, both visual (concealing/unconcealing) and auditory (non-sonorous/sonorous), at play in the relation between silence and speech. Even conceding that sound and silence are not interpreted in metaphysical terms, their relation through speech places them in what is traditionally called sensible and supersensible, respectively. In *The Event*, for example, the visual/aural coupling takes form in the resonating of beyng where "its soundless voice and its imageless conjuncture become perceptible."[10] The thinking of beyng co-responds in its "imageless saying."[11] Heidegger uses scare quotes to refer to this thinking as one that "can never claim 'the sensory,'" and that "does not need the sensory and images," unlike poetry's "imagistic" saying.[12] However, I would argue that it is not difficult to see how imagelessness and soundlessness can correlate with the supersensible on the one hand, and imagery and sonorous saying can correlate with the sensible on the other.

One could argue on Heidegger's behalf that the words "silence," "sound," and "speech" still transmit the transformative power of transitional thinking as it turns around their meanings toward the other beginning. In this sense, one could point out that their definitions are framed in terms of the appropriating-event, truth, beyng, and the word. Within this framework of interpretation, "silence" as the absence of sound, "sound" as acoustical vibration, and "speech" as the rational animal's instrument of expression and communication in articulate sounds prove to be inadequate. Such inadequacy would not necessarily entail that they are incorrect, but that they are not true, in the sense of revealing what is essential. However, I claim that those essential meanings could still be interpreted critically as metaphors that relate what is supersensible to what is sensible.[13]

Heidegger's idea of the earth in the fourfold perhaps illustrates his best attempt to infuse the transitional meanings of sound, silence, and speech with connotations of corporeality. As the self-secluding realm of closedness upon which the mortals dwell, it is the depth from which language blooms as the flower of the mouth and the homeland where the mother tongue has its roots. It grants "earthyness" to the sounding in the mouth of the mortals and to those future ones who "have an ear" for the stilling of the stillness.[14] Sounding itself takes place in the strife of earth and world, which reflects the tension of truth as the clearing-concealing of beyng. Da-sein shelters this truth in beings as beings and preserves the self-concealing, and this happens in the mouth of the mortals in their sonorous saying. However, I claim that the ear and the mouth in these depictions are at the site of the clearing, in which the human body must itself first be disclosed as such, and this happens in the sonorous saying. Put otherwise, the ear and the mouth of the living body presuppose the metaphorical ear and mouth. So, I claim that our lived experiences of hearing and speaking, in the flesh, as it were, are dis-located from the body proper. In this sense, Heidegger not only retains the distinction between the sensible and the supersensible but also conjures a new form of disharmony for our embodied existence. Thus, I claim that he fails to in-corporate in his philosophy the embodied experiences in his thoughts on silence.

In his *Black Notebooks*, Heidegger issues an illuminating self-critique regarding his treatment of embodiment in his *Fundamental Concepts of Metaphysics: World, Finitude, Solitude*. The question concerning the greatness of humans must be one that "bears silence" and "what we so name—the transience and the merely psycho-bodily—are to be taken in the extrinsic sense—of course without dealing *with it* (Mistake in . . . [GA29–30])."[15] In his view, then, his "mistake" was to focus explicitly on the fundamental mood of boredom in terms of lived and embodied experiences, which are extrinsic in the sense of being nonessential to the self-definition of human essence in its freedom. Such focus would accordingly preempt the reticent question into the greatness of humans in his view.

The *Heraclitus Seminar* offers further illumination on Heidegger's self-critique concerning the focus on what is "merely psycho-bodily." There, he reacts strongly to Eugen Fink's idea of the "ontic proximity" of the human to "the underground of all clearing." This proximity represents our relation to "the nightly ground" insofar as the human "belongs bodily to the earth and to the flowing of life." Furthermore, this is a "dark understanding" that "doesn't let itself be brought further to language." Heidegger criticizes two implications concerning our embodiment in this context. The first would diminish the (ontological) greatness of humans in their disclosive essence: "A human is embodied [*leibt*] only when he lives [*lebt*]. The body in your sense is to be understood thus. Thereby 'to live' is meant in the existential sense. Ontic proximity means no spatial proximity between two things, but a reduced openness, thus a human ontological moment. And nevertheless, you speak of an ontic proximity." The second implication would erase the abyssal differences between the human and the animal: "The bodily in the human is not something animalistic."[16]

When Fink reminds Heidegger that in his *Fundamental Concepts of Metaphysics*, he had called the animal "world-poor" and was thus "underway toward the affinity of the human with nature," Heidegger responds: "The body phenomenon is the most difficult problem." So, I maintain that, while he does not offer a solution to this most difficult problem, he continues to recoil from the embodiment of the human essence and its lived "earthyness." Significantly, he also subsumes here the issue of the "adequate constitution of the sound of speech" to this most difficult problem, and he argues that "[p]honetics thinks too physicalistically, when it does not see *phōnē* (speech) as voice in the correct manner."[17] In my critical conclusion, the sounds of speech are also disembodied in Heidegger's approach.

Furthermore, I maintain that Heidegger's interpretation of the body in effect closes off the possibility of developing a phenomenology of the lived *embodied* experiences that often accompany the silencing attunements, as when we feel uncanny and shudder in dread or when we are listless in profound boredom. It also closes off the possibility of exploring silence and the limits of language with regard to what Fink calls our "dark understanding" of the earth and the pulsating life. However, it is interesting to note that Heidegger did not disregard the fact of the "body's being born-by-mood," as when we say that "a stomachache puts a damper on the mood." Yet, he insisted that "[i]llness is not a disturbance of a biological process, but an historical happening of the human being, something that is grounded among other things in being-attuned."[18] (As I write in these times of the Coronavirus pandemic—a world "historical happening"—I would argue that a more adequate formulation is that it is not *only* a "disturbance of a biological process.")

I contend further that Heidegger's failure to in-corporate the body into his philosophical concept of silence also results in an erasure of the lived differences in human existence and, in particular, of the social, cultural, economic, and political powers that transmute and congeal these differences into disparities. The gender neutrality of Da-sein, the homogeneity of the *Volk* as a "We," and the one world of the *Mitdasein* (being-there-with) are ideas that obliterate the embodied differences at the same time that they occlude the body altogether and exclude the bodies that differ. However, Heidegger's jingoism, which is explicit in many of his public essays and lectures, as well as the antisemitism that he expressed predominantly in his private writings, are tendencies that are compatible with the erasure of the lived differences precisely because they too occlude the body.[19]

Heidegger interpreted his own "-isms" as matters of the *spirit* or of historical Da-sein, instead of the human body and its biology, physiology, and physiognomy.[20] In his 1949 Bremen Lecture, "the production of corpses in the gas chambers and extermination camps" is thus for him another instance of *Ge-stell* (the en-framing essence of modern technology), comparable to the mechanized food industry and the production of the H-bomb.[21] Focusing on the "[h]undreds of thousands who die in mass," Heidegger also suggests that it is *Ge-stell* that distorts their death, so that they do not "die" (*sterben*) in the sense of "carrying out death in its essence," but instead "perish" (*kommen um*), are "put down" (*werden umgelegt*), "become pieces of inventory of a standing reserve in the fabrication of corpses," and are "unobtrusively liquidated" (*liquidiert*) in "annihilation camps." Such is the ending here of the human who is "not yet" the mortal—the one who is "capable of carrying . . . out death" and is "endeared to the essence of death" in embracing its mortality in anticipatory resoluteness.[22] I would argue that an alternative approach that incorporates the lived body could register the silencing experiences of those whose bodies suffer stigmatization, exclusion, oppression, and extermination, it could be attuned to the dignity of the human being, and it could let the different voices be heard.

9.2. STRIKING CHORDS BETWEEN THE RETICENT CO-RESPONDENCE OF POETRY AND THINKING, THE METAPHYSICAL SILENCE OF MYSTICISM, AND THE LOUD CHATTER OF EVERYDAYNESS

Heidegger develops a scale of silence that places poetry and thinking at the highest level of attunement, with their characteristic hearkening, keeping silent, and reticence. Perhaps, at a much lower level of attunement, we may find philosophers, like Herder, and poets, like George, who have a sense of the deeper silences, but are deafened by the metaphysics of objective presence. Given later Heidegger's dismissal of what is mystical as metaphysical and his critique of onto-theology, it seems that the mystical approach to silence is another instance of the mishearing (*verhören*) that characterizes traditional philosophy and theology.[23] Because he also disparages everyday discourse in its fundamental failure to hear (*Überhören*) and not wanting to hear (*Nichthörenwollen*), it is evident that the loud idle talk is banished from Heidegger's scale of silence.[24] So, I claim that, in effect, he allows only for one authentic or genuine form of attunement with the deeper silences.

I also maintain that Heidegger's depiction of the primeval and primordial silences as autonomous forces and originary sites of unconcealedness aims to capture certain experiences of the power of silence, but not all, for he sets narrow parameters. He stipulates what is experienced, namely, the primeval silence that belongs to the stillness and the primordial silencing that pertains to the word. In this vein, he characterizes the experiences as appropriative moments of the "experiencing" (*Erfahrung*) of beyng and of the "essential experiencing" (*Wesenserfahrung*) of language.[25] Accordingly, he takes pains to distinguish them from lived experiences of beings, and especially from cognitive, conceptual, or empirical experiences of objects. So, he also stipulates how the experiencing can occur: only in the mindful hearkening to the silent truth of beyng and the word in the appropriating-event.

Evidently, the thinking and poetic experiencing as Heidegger describes them are not what are traditionally regarded as mystical experiences of silence, for example, of the silence of god or of the godhead, of the divine silence, and of the profoundly spiritual and sublime silence that many world religions include in their doctrines. These mystical experiences commonly refer to direct experiences of the soul or the spirit, to spiritual revelations, intuitions, or insights, or to a union or a communion with a personal deity, a spiritual truth, or an ultimate reality that transcends the senses and the intellect. Cognizant of these meanings, Heidegger emphasizes that beyng " 'is' not 'God'" and "'is' never the god," but "'is' before the gods and humans" and "'*is*' more inaugural than any decision about these."[26] He also categorically states that the word "mystic" "does not count" as a word that meets "the attuning of the voice of beyng" because the "thinking of being goes before all theology and philo-sophy, that is, metaphysics."[27] Moreover, he dismisses the "delight of the 'mystical' regard that simply remains ensnared in the representation of something that presences" as a way in which beyng is "able to be experienced."[28]

I will leave open the question of whether Heidegger's characterizations adequately capture the mystical experiences described in the world's religious and spiritual traditions.[29] I would like to focus instead on the fact that he constantly places the words "mystic" and "mystical" in scare quotes, for my sense is that this leaves open the possibility of a mysticism that is not ensnared in metaphysics. It is perhaps telling that Heidegger says nothing about the original meaning of the word "mystic" when he places it in scare quotes. It comes from the ancient Greek "*mystikos*," which means "of mysteries" and this meaning comes from the word "*mystes*" or "initiate." What is mystical in its deeper sense would thereby have its hidden ground in the mystery of beyng that initiates from the stillness and has in poets and thinkers its silent and reticent initiates. The word, as the soundless peal of the stillness would be the initiatory call, the mysterious message of beyng. I claim that, in this special sense, Heidegger's words on silence could be themselves characterized as mystical sayings of the crossing. His private manuscripts could thus be seen as mystical meditative exercises that often take on the form of repetitive incantations. The alliterative formulations of etymological cognates that mark his own style of sonorous saying could also include the mystical aim of attuning us to the deeper silences.[30] However, these are positive possibilities that he silently passes over when he questions mysticism and emphatically marks its distance from the authentic thinking and poetizing of beyng.

I maintain that Heidegger's positive regard for the language of the homeland that is handed down in the tradition of a people and through its lore opens up a way to counterbalance his continual disparagement of the everyday discourse as loud chatter. He attributes to poetry the inaugural saying and often portrays its inevitable decline in the everyday idle talk. However, it is in one and same mother tongue that he sees the "preservation [*Bewahrung*]" of this poetic saying and the "safeguarding [*Verwahrung*] of the new possibilities of the already spoken language," which "itself contains and grants the unspoken."[31] Thus, I would argue that the language of the venerable tradition that shelters what is unspoken cannot be completely out of tune with silence.

The possibility of an authentic silence in everyday discourse would appear to be a contradiction in terms for Heidegger. Yet, he does allow for rare instances in everyday speaking with one another that are neither idle talk nor objectifying speech.[32] He also mentions a few cases of everyday *silence* that have the marks of authenticity (in the general sense of the proper mindfulness of being/beyng). One case pertains to what I have already identified as the "secondary" form of authentic keeping silent and reticence of being-in-the-world in dialogues with one another, which presupposes the reticent resoluteness of Da-sein as a self.[33] Another case regards the *Volk* as a "community" that is "silent in the great work," which presupposes the individual's exposedness to beings through the language.[34] However, in the latter case, poetry and thinking already have the foundational roles and thus provide the more originary attunements to silence. Therefore, all possible attunements of the "We" and the "Self" remain secondary in this case.

I also argue that Heidegger's general distinction between authentic and inauthentic discourse or speech becomes increasingly problematic as its application widens from Da-sein's truth to the truth of beyng. The former concerns the possibilities of self-disclosure as being-towards-death and in its being-in-the-world. The latter pertains to the clearing-concealing of beyng in the possibilities of the event of appropriation of the mortals in the fourfold of the world. How any mortal, even one among the few and the rare, can adjudicate on the saying that is most proper to beyng presents a serious challenge to the coherence of Heidegger's distinction and hierarchization. His tendency to conflate essence with authenticity and unessence with inauthenticity only exacerbates this problem of his stepping over the limits of what he defines as the word of beyng.[35] Yet, without the questionable scales of beyng and essence, the mystical and everyday forms of attunement to the deeper silences would simply be different from, but neither lesser than nor secondary to, nor necessarily based on the thinking and poetic attunements.[36]

9.3. THE SILENT DUET OF THE SONOROUS MORTALS AND THE HINTING IMMORTALS AGAINST THE CACOPHONY OF LANGUAGELESS ANIMALS AND THE LOUDNESS OF THE MODERN TECHNOLOGICAL AGE

In Heidegger's depictions of the fourfold, the mortals who dwell upon the earth, beneath the sky, and in the en-counter with the immortals are the only beings whose essence is determined by language in its essence as the soundless saying. I claim that the need of this soundless saying for the mortals to co-respond in their sonorous speech sets the dominant tone for all forms of sounds and silences within the world as the unitary fourfold. The showing of the world and its regions in the word-sounds of the mortals takes form through and is determined by the as-structure, which the mortals themselves apply in their self-definition as mortals. Put otherwise, there would be no world at all without the "there" of beyng in the appropriating-event, without the appropriation of the being that discloses itself in its mortality, by showing to itself its death *as* death.

Heidegger's characterizations of the immortals or the gods in terms of their indigence (*Notschaft*) highlight their need (*Not*) for beyng. However, beyng itself needs the mortals, who belong to it by hearkening and submitting to its silent voice and are thereby the stewards who preserve its truth. Though the en-countering of mortals in their stewardship and the immortals in their indigence defines each in their essence toward and against one another, only the mortals are appropriated for the resounding of the stillness. The gods are silent, even when they address and call the mortals toward their essence as the sonorous sayers. The hinting and beckoning by the immortals takes place in soundlessness, for the gods themselves cannot speak in word-sounds. In this sense, their silence is not verbal as such and their saying is not sonorous. Yet, it is still a saying, that is, the gods show something in the manner of pointing to it, wordlessly, without naming it, for that is the founding task of the poets among the mortals.

If we think about the fourfold in terms of the structure (*Gefüge*) of the clearing-concealing of beyng that gathers fitting together (*Fügung*) the regions into the unity of the world, then the gods fit into the realm of what is divine, sacred, and holy in beyng itself. Yet, only the mortals fit into the sonorous disclosure of the world as world, which *includes* the godly realm. In Heidegger's depiction of the beyng-historical fourfold in the age of machination, the godlessness, the absconding of the gods, and the passing by of the last god must first be experienced in Da-sein for the decision concerning the gods' advent or absconding to occur. It is in Da-sein's great stillness that this decisive experience can occur as Da-sein hearkens to the deeper silences of beyng and the word. Heidegger thus admonishes us, "Ask beyng! And in its silence, in the inceptual essence of the word, the god answers."[37] Yet, this answer itself is soundless. Moreover, it can only become sonorous through Da-sein, who not only has the possibility of deciding about the gods but is also the one who can *name* them, if these possibilities are granted to it in the appropriating-event.[38] I claim that, in this sense, the silent calls and answers of the gods are determined as such through the linguistic essence of the mortals. In the silent duet of the mortals and the immortals, there is ultimately one dominant voice. In fact, there is only one sounding voice, for neither the gods nor the animals are capable of sonorous speech.[39]

In the 1934 summer course *Logic as the Question Concerning Language*, Heidegger offered a lyrical description of the "world-forming power" of language that evokes some of his later characterizations of the fourfold in the age of machination, but without mentioning the gods:

> The loveliness of the valley and the menace of the mountain and of the raging sea, the sublimity of the stars, the absorption of the plant and the ensnarement of the animal, the calculated speed of machines and the severity of the historical action, the harnessed frenzy of the created work, the cold boldness of the questioning that knows, the hardened sobriety of labor and the discretion of the heart—all that *is* language; wins or loses being only in the event of language.[40]

The world disclosed by language—the earth with its waters, stones, plants, and animals, the sky with its stars, the mortals in their creative, steadfast, and courageous reticence, and the framing or en-framing essence of technology in the history of beyng—are all anticipated here. Language is also what distinguishes human existence from animal life.[41] Animals live, only humans exist.[42] The as-structure is decisive in the distinction between the human being and the ensnared animal: "Beings *as* beings do not encounter the animal; beings are neither manifest nor concealed to the animal."[43]

Shortly after the 1934 course on logic, Heidegger speaks of the gods and the demigods in relation to the mortals of Mother Earth in his interpretation of Hölderlin's hymns "Germania" and "The Rhein." Though an eagle speaks in "Germania," it is as the messenger of the gods who speaks of language with the humans, so that in this sonorous dialogue they disclose language in language. However, the animal as such, in the "captivated entanglement" that marks its "essential otherness" from the human, is excluded from the realm of language.[44] I maintain that this would entail that just as the animal is languageless, it is "silenceless" as well. In this sense, the animal is essentially incapable of speech; it cannot speak in word-sounds, talk or discourse, say or tell, show or disclose, veil and unveil, hear and keep silent—in the sense that Heidegger gives to these terms.

In Heidegger's confrontation with Herder in his 1939 summer course *On the Essence of Language*, the animal reappears "captivated and dazed." It is denied even the metaphysically defined possibility of an "animal language" consisting of the "sounding" or "resounding of sensations."[45] In fact, Heidegger denies to the animal the capacity for language all along, throughout the significant changes in his definitions of "language" and "world."

In Heidegger's 1929–30 lecture course *The Fundamental Concepts of Metaphysics: World, Finitude, Solitude*, we find an extensive discussion of the concept of "world" through the theses of the stone as worldless, the animal in its captivation as world-poor, and the human in its freedom as world-forming. With "world" defined in terms of "the *manifestness of beings as such and as a whole*," the pre-predicative as-structure in its relation to the understanding of the being of beings plays a key role in marking the essential distinction between the human, the animal, and the stone.[46] Thus, in the example of a lizard basking on a rock in the sun, Heidegger claims that neither the sun nor the rock is given for the lizard "*as*" sun and rock, but "are just lizard-things for the lizard."[47] The connection between the as-structure and language, which he defines here as "something that belongs to the essence of man in his finitude," is based on the understanding of being.[48] In this (derivative) sense, language does not belong to the essence of the animal because "linguistic naming, and all language, always already involves an understanding of beings."[49]

Moreover, Heidegger claims that, while the sounds that the animal produces do "designate something," they "are not words, they have no meaning, they cannot give anything as meaningful."[50] In fact, the only way animal sounds can be said to have meaning at all is through *our* interpretation:

> The animal can perhaps neither observe itself, nor communicate any such observations to us. And even if the animal expresses itself and announces itself, as it seems to us, in a variety of expressive sounds and movements, it is we who must first interpret and analyze such forms of expression.[51]

At the same time, Heidegger does concede that animals communicate with one another at least (as in the case of the bees that "communicate information about newly discovered feeding places by performing a sort of dance in the hive").[52] Presumably, our ability to interpret animal expression is linked to the fact that humans can "transpose" themselves into the animal's sphere, which is potentially transposable for humans, unlike the case of the stone.[53] However, Heidegger discards the possibility of the *animal* being able to transpose itself into the human world. Even the dog that is our domestic pet is not with us in the manner of "*existing-with*, because a dog does not exist but merely lives," so that there is a "going along with . . . a transposedness, and yet not."[54]

In marking the abyssal differences between Da-sein in its existence, the animal in its life, and the stone in its mere being at hand, Heidegger also focused on death: The stone in its absorption "does not even have the possibility of dying," because "it is never alive."[55] The animal in its captivation "cannot die in the sense in which dying is ascribed to humans, but can only come to an end."[56] Only Da-sein in its understanding of being is in the manner of "being toward death" and "comports himself somehow or other towards death, that is, toward *his* death," understanding his Da-sein at its "most extreme possibility."[57] In the later essays on the essence of language, the connection between death and the as-structure is fully based on language: "Mortals are they who can experience death as death. Animals cannot do so. But animals cannot speak either. The essential relation between death and language flashes up before us, but remains still unthought."[58] In this sense, "human speech" is "the speech of the mortals."[59]

I claim that, in the end, the animals are captivated and ensnared by *Heidegger's* dim views of them as the beings that live and perish on the earth of the fourfold and are separated by an abyss from the mortals in their languagelessness. From this speciesist perspective, the sonorousness of animals is itself a cacophony, meaningful only for the mortals and through the as-structure of the word, which determines only the essence of the human being. Yet, I maintain that it is questionable that their cries and shrieks are mere sounds without meaning, even if we were to concede that they are abyssally different from the word-sounds of the mortals. Animals are able to communicate with one another, so their sounds and silences must bear some sort of intrinsic meaning. I would argue that it is also questionable that no animal can experience its death as death, though evidently the as-structure would not be verbal. Perhaps we would be better at letting the earth be the earth, if we tried to transpose ourselves into the animal's intrinsically meaningful experiences, including that of its own extreme possibility.

In Heidegger's depiction of the age of machination, the "great stillness must first come over the world for the earth."[60] This is a call for the few who in their "keeping silent" and "restraint" prepare for the appropriation of Da-sein as the "sustaining" of the strife of the earth and the world, which "has its essence in the sheltering of the truth of beyng."[61] In this vein, Heidegger also poses the urgent question, "Why is the earth silent at this destruction?"

and he bemoans the abandonment of nature to gigantism and machination.[62] At issue is whether the human being will be "masterful enough" for the "transition to the renewal of the world out of the saving of the earth."[63] The threat to the human being in this darkness is instead "*the transition to the technologized animal*."[64] The human is thus in the throes, with this consummation of the metaphysical rational animal, which chatters noisily in the modern technological language of unessence—the "language-machine."[65] The loudness of the epoch of gigantism and machination thus threatens to frame by gathering together (in the sense of *Ge-stell*) all of the possibilities of speech and silence.

I believe that many of Heidegger's prophecies of doom concerning the framing essence of modern technology unfortunately seem to be confirmed in our "Information Age." However, he also shared his visions of hope in the saving power of language, the reticent mindfulness of the poets and thinkers, and the fundamental disposition of "releasement" (*Gelassenheit*) toward things. In releasement, we say "'yes' and at the same time 'no'" in "our comportment toward technology," by simultaneously letting technological things come into our everydayness and "leave them outside, that is, let them alone, as things which are nothing absolute but remain dependent on something higher."[66] Though Heidegger allowed for very few instances of authentic speech and silence in the everyday, I believe that releasement with regard to the digital devices that prevail in our daily lives today could afford us more possibilities for mindfulness and quiescence than he envisioned.

NOTES

1. For a different view, see: Niall Keane, "The Silence of the Origin: Philosophy in Transition and the Essence of Thinking" in *Research in Phenomenology*, Vol. 43 (2013): 27–48. Keane claims that "a perfect silence" is an "impossibility," given the need and use of the essence of language for mortal speech to "shatter" its stillness (33). However, I believe that this characterization can be misleading, as it would imply that the stillness is somehow imperfect and that its need is a lack. In my rendition, the totality of its silence is based on the absolute soundlessness of the stillness understood as a positive fullness.

2. See section 7.1 for my remarks on this dif-ference.

3. In Wanda Torres Gregory, *Heidegger's Path to Language* (Lanham, Maryland: Lexington Books, 2016), I formulate a similar charge against the "phonetic reductionism" focused on his concept of language (115–17).

4. Perhaps one of the most famous statements on music and the impossibility of silence comes from American composer and music theorist John Cage, whose controversial 1952 composition *4′33″* consists of 4 minutes and 33 seconds in which musicians do *not* play their instruments. For further philosophical discussions of

Cage's and other theories on music and silence, see: Steven L. Bindemann, ed., *Silence in Philosophy, Literature and Art* (Leiden; Boston: Brill Rodopi, 2017), chapters 3 and 4; and Isabella van Elferen and Sven Raeymaekers, "Silent Dark: The Orders of Silence" in *Journal for Cultural Research*, Vol. 19, Nr. 3 (2015): 262–73. For a phenomenology of silence in relation to music that proposes to go beyond the Husserlian and Heideggerean phenomenologies, see: Don Idhe, *Listening and Voice: Phenomenologies of Silence* (New York: State University of New York Press, 2nd ed. 2007), especially chapter 2.

5. Martin Heidegger, "The Origin of the Work of Art" in *Poetry, Language, Thought*, trans. Albert Hofstadter (New York: Harper & Row, 1971), 19 / GA5, 3.

6. Heidegger, *The Principle of Reason*, trans. Reginald Lilly (Bloomington and Indianapolis: Indiana University Press, 1996), 47 / SG, 86–88.

7. This does not rule out many thought-provoking links between these arts and silence. For example, with regard to architecture, van Elferen and Raeymaekers discuss the phenomenology of being in the "anechoic chamber" or "dead-space," which is a room that blocks all outside sounds and does not allow inside sound to reverberate. Van Elferen and Raeymaekers, "Silent Dark: The Orders of Silence," 265. See also: Max Picard, "Poetry and Silence" and "The Plastic Arts and Silence" in *A World of Silence*, trans. Stanley Godwin (Wichita, Kansas: Eighth Day Press, 2002). Max Picard was a Swiss Catholic theologian who was influenced by Gabriel Marcel, Heidegger, Hölderlin, and Rainer Maria Rilke, among others, in his meditations on the relation between silence and many other dimensions of life, including poetry and the plastic arts.

8. Heidegger, "The Origin of the Work of Art," 73–74 / GA5, 60–62.

9. Heidegger, *Contributions to Philosophy (Of the Event)*, trans. Richard Rojcewicz and Daniela Vallega-Neu (Bloomington and Indianapolis: Indiana University Press, 2012), 484 / GA65, 502–03.

10. Heidegger, *The Event*, trans. Richard Rojcewicz (Bloomington and Indianapolis: Indiana University Press, 2013), 65 / GA71, 78–79.

11. See, for example, ibid., 34 / GA71, 43; 248 / GA71, 285; 289 / GA71, 333.

12. Cf. ibid., 189 / GA71, 220; §374.

13. In this regard, I am disagreeing with David Norwell Smith's argument that Heidegger's idea of the hearkening and speech of the mortals is invested with corporeal meanings that overcome the metaphysical sensible/supersensible distinction. David Norwell Smith, *Sounding / Silence. Martin Heidegger at the Limits of Poetics* (New York: Fordham University Press, 2013.)

14. Cf. Heidegger, "Hebel-Friend of the House," trans. B.V. Flotz and M. Heim in *Contemporary German Philosophy* 3(1983): 89–101 / HH; Heidegger, "Sprache und Heimat" in GA13; Heidegger, "The Nature of Language" in *On the Way to Language*, trans. Peter D. Hertz (New York: Harper & Row, 1971), 101 / US, 208; and Heidegger, *Contributions to Philosophy (Of the Event)*, 124 / GA65, 112.

15. Heidegger, *Ponderings II–VI: Black Notebooks 1931–1938*, trans. Richard Rojcewicz (Bloomington and Indianapolis: Indiana University Press, 2016), 60–61 / GA94 II–VI, 80.

16. Heidegger, *Heraclitus Seminar*, trans. Charles H. Seiber (Evanston: Northwestern University Press, 1994), 145–47 / GA15, 235–37. See section 9.3 for my discussion of problem of abyss in terms of the languageless of the animal.

17. Ibid., 146 / GA15, 236.

18. Heidegger, *Logic as the Question Concerning the Essence of Language*, trans. Wanda Torres Gregory and Yvonne Unna (Albany, New York: State University of New York Press, 2009), 127 / GA38, 153.

19. Berel Lang, *Heidegger's Silence* (Ithaca and London: Cornell University Press, 1996) captures this issue by critically linking Heidegger's silence concerning the "Jewish Question" (specifically, in relation to the Holocaust) to the status that he assigns to the *Volk* on the basis of "*spiritual grounds*" in his public and philosophical writings (chapter 2). Adam Knowles, *Heidegger's Fascist Affinities: A Politics of Silence* (Stanford, California: Stanford University Press, 2019) exposes more recent connections between Heidegger's antisemitism and silence in his public and private writings (especially in his *Black Notebooks*). For critiques that focus on what I label Heidegger's "failure of in-corporation" with regard to the silencing of bodies in terms of gender, see, for example, Luce Irigaray, "To Conceive Silence" in *To be Two*, trans. Monique M. Rhodes and Marco F. Cocito-Monoc (New York: Routledge, 2001); and Jacques Derrida, "Geschlecht: Sexual Difference, Ontological Difference" in *Feminist Interpretations of Martin Heidegger,* Nancy J. Holland and Patricia Huntington, eds. (University Park, Pennsylvania: The Pennsylvania State University Press, 2001). In Torres Gregory, *Heidegger's Path to Language*, I issue a similar critique of his "dis-location" of the body, but as part of what I label "linguistic preternaturalism" there (199–200).

20. A prime example of this focus on the spirit and the historical Da-sein is visible in his 1933 rectoral address: Heidegger, "The Self-Assertion of the German University," in *Martin Heidegger and National Socialism*, Gunther Neske and Emil Kettering, eds. (New York: Paragon House, 1990). Translation of Heidegger, "Die Selbstbehauptung der deutschen Universität" (Breslau: Korn, 1933). See also: Heidegger, *Logic as the Question Concerning the Essence of* Language, §14 / GA38, §14; 127 / GA38, 153. Jacques Derrida, *Of Spirit: Heidegger and the Question,* trans. Geoffrey Bennington and Rachel Bowlby (Chicago: The University of Chicago Press, 1989), critically links "the *Geist* [that] is always haunted by its *Geist*" in Heidegger to a form of "metaphysics of race" that tries to demarcate itself from a "biologism of race" (39–40, 73–74). In *Heidegger's Silence,* Lang critically analyzes Heidegger's endorsement of the *Volk* principle on "*spiritual*" as opposed to "biological" grounds (26). Lang also argues that Heidegger's own narrow definition of antisemitism as a biological racism does not resolve the issue of his antisemitism and endorsement of Nazi ideology (chapter 4).

21. Heidegger, *Bremen and Freiburg Lectures. Insight into That Which Is and Basic Principles of Thinking*, trans. Andrew J. Mitchell (Bloomington: Indiana University Press, 2012), 27 / GA79, 27.

22. Ibid., 53 / GA79, 56.

23. Heidegger, *Hölderlin's Hymns "Germania" and "The Rhein,"* trans. William McNeill and Julia Anne Ireland (Indiana: Indiana University Press, 2014), 40 / GA39,

41. See also: Heidegger, "The Problem of a Non-Objectifying Thinking and Speaking in Today's Theology" in *The Piety of Thinking*, trans. J. G. Hart and J. C. Maraldo (Bloomington: Indiana University Press, 1976) / PT.

24. Ibid., §14b. In Torres Gregory, *Heidegger's Path to Language*, I make similar critiques, but I focus on his *linguistic* "anthropocentrism," "foundationalism," and "prejudices" (100–106).

25. Heidegger, GA74, 18–19.

26. Ibid., 22–27. Cf. ibid., 37, 39, 59, 60.

27. Ibid., 29. Cf. ibid., 93.

28. Ibid., 149. Yet, Heidegger argued against applying this view to the mystic Meister Eckhardt's understanding of God and soul. See Heidegger, "The Thing" in *Poetry, Language, Thought*, trans. Albert Hofstadter (New York: Harper & Row, 1971), 176–77 / VA, 178.

29. This is a question that is complicated by Heidegger's expert knowledge of the mysticism of Meister Eckhardt and his familiarity with East-Asian philosophies that include mystical doctrines and practices, such as Chinese Daoism and Zen Buddhism. For a comparison of the later Heidegger's ideas of beyng and language with Meister Eckhardt mysticism, see: John D. Caputo *The Mystical Element in Heidegger's Thought* (New York: Fordham University Press, 1978, 1986, 2nd rev. ed.), 166–72, 224–25. Caputo argues that Heidegger is not a mystic, but his definition of mysticism aligns with what *Heidegger* would call "metaphysical" or "onto-theological" mysticism. Reinhard May, *Heidegger's Hidden Sources*, trans. Graham Parks (New York: Routledge, 1989) develops a scathing critique of Heidegger's appropriation of East-Asian philosophies. Elisabeth Feist Hirsch, "Martin Heidegger and the East" in *Philosophy East and West*, Vol. 20, Nr. 3 (July 1970): 247–63, offers a clear summary of points of comparison (on silence, 216–17) between Heidegger and Asian philosophies for the non-specialist.

30. For similar characterizations of Heidegger's style during his later period, see: Francisco Gonzalez, "And the Rest is *Sigetik*: Silencing Logic and Dialectic in Heidegger's *Beiträge zur Philosophie*" in *Research in Phenomenology*, Vol. 38 (2008): 358–91; and Daniela Vallega-Neu, "Heidegger's Reticence: From *Contributions* to Das *Ereignis* and toward *Gelassenheit*" in *Research in Phenomenology*, Vol. 45 (2015): 1–32.

31. Heidegger, "Traditional Language and Technological Language," trans. Wanda Torres Gregory" in *Journal of Philosophical Research*, Vol. XXIII, 1998: 129–145, 142 / UT, 27.

32. Cf. Heidegger, *Being and Time*, 231 / SZ, 165; *Logic as the Question Concerning the Essence of Language*, GA38, §31; *Hölderlin's Hymns "Germania" and "The Rhein,"* GA39, §7.j.; Heidegger, "Traditional Language and Technological Language" / UT; Heidegger, "Hebel-Friend of the House," trans. B. V. Flotz and M. Heim, *Contemporary German Philosophy* 3(1983): 89–101 / HH ; and Heidegger, *The Piety of Thinking*, trans. J. G. Hart and J. C. Maraldo (Bloomington: Indiana University Press, 1976), 27–28 / PT, 43. See also: Heidegger, *Country Path Conversations*, trans. Bret Davis (Bloomington: Indiana University Press, 2010) / GA77. The conversations that take place in this work do not occur between poets and

thinkers, yet are profound dialogues that certainly do not fit his characterizations of idle talk.

33. See section 1.1 for my discussion of Heidegger's earlier view of the primary and secondary forms of authentic discourse.

34. See section 2.2 and section 3.1 for my discussion of Heidegger's earlier view of the possibilities of genuine silence for the *Volk*.

35. See section 1.1, section 2.1, and section 3.1 for my examination of different instances of Heidegger's conflation of essence and authenticity. In Torres Gregory, *Heidegger's Path to Language,* I develop a similar critique, claiming that he "violates his own principle of linguistic immanence" and "ends up vaulting the limits of language" that he traces from within (184).

36. See: Bernard P. Dauenhauer *Silence: The Phenomenon and its Ontological Significance* (Bloomington, Indiana: Indiana University Press, 1980), chapter 5. Dauenhauer also claims that authentic silence and discourse are restricted to their creative modes in Heidegger's later works. Dauenhauer argues for his own interpretation of silence as an intentional phenomenon that is always somehow connected with discourse, but has ontological significance as a positive phenomenon that is not simply correlative with discourse.

37. Heidegger, *The History of Beyng*, trans. William McNeill and Jeffrey Powell (Bloomington, Indiana: Indiana University Press, 2015), 179 / GA69, 211–12; see also, ibid., 28 / GA69, 30–31.

38. Ibid., 121 / GA69, 141–42. See also: Heidegger, *Contributions to Philosophy (Of the Event)*, 408 / GA65, 423.

39. Heidegger, *The Fundamental Concepts of Metaphysics: World, Finitude, Solitude*, 238 / GA29/30, 346. In Torres Gregory, *Heidegger's Path to Language,* my contention is that Heidegger "does not manage to overcome the anthropological speciesism of metaphysics" (174; cf. ibid., 200, 208), but I propose an alternative bio-linguistic model to Heidegger's denial of the as-structure in the animal experience (211–14).

40. Heidegger, *Logic as the Question Concerning the Essence of Language*, 140 / GA38, 168–69.

41. Ibid., 119 / GA38, 144.

42. Ibid., 112 / GA38, 135.

43. Ibid., 131 / GA38, 158. Jacques Derrida, "Heidegger's Ear: Philopolemonology (*Geschlecht IV*)." trans. John P. Leavey, Jr. in *Reading Heidegger: Commemorations*, ed. John Sallis (Bloomington and Indianapolis: Indiana University Press, 1993) captures this issue well: "Whether a matter of feet, eye, sex, or ear, the Heideggerean phenomenology of Da-sein's body, in what is more original or more necessary in that phenomenology, supposes precisely the phenomenological as such or the phenomenological 'as such'"(173).

44. Heidegger, *Hölderlin's Hymns "Germania" and "The Rhein,"* 68 / GA39, 75.

45. Heidegger, *On the Essence of Language. The Metaphysics of Language and the Essencing of the Word. Concerning Herder's Treatise* On the Origin of Language, trans. Wanda Torres Gregory and Yvonne Unna (Albany, New York: State University of New York Press, 2004) / GA85, sections 2, 17, 73.

46. Heidegger, *The Fundamental Concepts of Metaphysics: World, Finitude, Solitude*, trans. William McNeill and Nicholas Walker (Bloomington: Indiana University Press, 1995), 301 / GA29/30, 435.
47. Ibid., 197 / GA9/30, 291. See also ibid., 247 / GA29/30, 360.
48. Ibid., 237 / GA29/30, 346.
49. Ibid., 259 / GA29/30, 376.
50. Ibid., 308 / GA29/30, 446.
51. Ibid., 179 / GA29/30, 266.
52. Ibid., 186 / GA29/30, 274.
53. Ibid., §50.
54. Ibid., 210 / GA29/30, 308.
55. Ibid., 179 / GA29/30, 265.
56. Ibid., 267 / GA29/30, 388.
57. Ibid., 294 / GA29/30, 425–26.
58. Heidegger, "The Nature of Language," 107 / US, 215.
59. Heidegger, "Language," 208 / US, 30.
60. Heidegger, *Contributions to Philosophy (Of the Event)*, 54 / GA65, 34.
61. Ibid. Cf. ibid., 111 / GA65, 96.
62. Ibid., 277 / GA65, 277–78. Cf. ibid., 121 / GA65, 108.
63. Ibid., 400 / GA65, 412.
64. Ibid., 113 / GA65, 98.
65. Heidegger, "Hebel-Friend of the House," trans. B. V. Flotz and M. Heim, *Contemporary German Philosophy*, Vol. 3(1983): 89–101 / HH.
66. Heidegger, "Memorial Address," in *Discourse on Thinking*, trans. John M. Anderson and E. Hans Freund (New York: Harper and Row, 1966), 54 / G, 25–26.

Bibliography

Absher, Brandon. "Speaking of Being: Language, Speech, and Silence in *Being and Time*." In *The Journal of Speculative Philosophy*, 30, Nr. 2 (2016): 204–231.

Bindemann, Steven L., ed. *Silence in Philosophy, Literature and Art*. Leiden; Boston: Brill Rodopi, 2017.

Caputo, John D. *The Mystical Element in Heidegger's Thought*. New York: Fordham University Press, 1978, 1986, 2nd rev. ed.

Dauenhauer, B. *Silence: The Phenomenon and its Ontological Significance*. Bloomington: Indiana University Press, 1980.

Derrida, Jacques. "Geschlecht: Sexual Difference, Ontological Difference." In *Feminist Interpretations of Martin Heidegger*. Edited by Holland Nancy J. and Patricia Huntington. University Park, Pennsylvania: The Pennsylvania State University Press, 2001.

———. "Heidegger's Ear: Philopolemology (*Geschlecht IV*)." Translated by John P. Leavey, Jr. In *Reading Heidegger: Commemorations*. Edited by John Sallis. Bloomington: Indiana University Press, 1993.

———. *Of Spirit: Heidegger and the Question*. Translated by Geoffrey Bennington and Rachel Bowlby. Chicago: The University of Chicago Press, 1989.

Feist Hirsch, Elisabeth. "Martin Heidegger and the East." In *Philosophy East and West*, 20, No. 3 (July, 1970): 247–63.

Gonzalez, Francisco J. "And the Rest is *Sigetik*: Silencing Logic and Dialectic in Heidegger's *Beiträge zur Philosophie*." In *Research in Phenomenology*, 38 (2008): 358–391.

Hanly, Peter. "Marking Silence: Heidegger and Herder on Word and Origin." In *Studia Philosophiae Christianae*, 49, Nr. 4 (2013): 69–86.

Heidegger, Martin. *Aus der Erfahrung des Denkens*, *Gesamtausgabe*, Vol. 13. Edited by Herrmann Heidegger. Frankfurt am Main: Klostermann, 1983.

———. *Being and Time*. Translated by John Macquarrie and Edward Robinson. New York: Harper and Row, 1962. Translation of Martin Heidegger, *Sein und Zeit*. Tübingen: Niemeyer, 1927; 16th ed. 1986.

———. *Being and Truth.* Translated by Gregory Fried and Richard Polt. Bloomington: Indiana University Press, 2010. Translation of Martin Heidegger, *Gesamtausgabe*, Vol. 36/37, *Sein und Wahrheit. 1. Die Grundfrage der Philosophie. 2. Vom Wesen der Wahrheit.* Edited by Hartmut Tietjen. Frankfurt am Main: Klostermann, 2001.

———. *Bremen and Freiburg Lectures. Insight into That Which Is and Basic Principles of Thinking.* Translated by Andrew J. Mitchell. Bloomington: Indiana University Press, 2012. Translation of *Gesamtausgabe*, Vol. 79, *Bremer und Freiburger Vorträge. 1. Einblick in das was ist. 2. Grundsätze des Denkens.* Edited by Petra Jaeger. Frankfurt am Main: Klostermann, 1994.

———. *Contributions to Philosophy (Of the Event).* Translated by Richard Rojcewicz and Daniela Vallega-Neu. Bloomington: Indiana University Press, 2012. Translation of Martin Heidegger, *Gesamtausgabe*, Vol. 65, *Beiträge zur Philosophie (Vom Ereignis).* Edited by Friedrich-Wilhelm von Herrmann. Frankfurt am Main: Klostermann, 1989; 2nd rev. ed. 1994.

———. *Country Path Conversations.* Translated by Bret Davis. Bloomington: Indiana University Press, 2010. Translation of Martin Heidegger, *Gesamtausgabe*, Vol. 77, *Feldweg-Gespräche.* Edited by Ingrid Schüßler. Frankfurt am Main: Klostermann, 1995; 2nd revised ed., 2007.

———. *Discourse on Thinking.* Translated by John M. Anderson and E. Hans Freund. New York: Harper and Row, 1966. Translation of Martin Heidegger, *Gelassenheit.*

———. *Early Greek Thinking.* Translated by David Ferrell Krell and Frank A. Capuzzi. New York: Harper & Row, 1974.

———. *Gelassenheit.* Pfullingen: Neske, 1959.

———. "Hebel-Friend of the House." Translated by B. V. Flotz and M. Heim. *Contemporary German Philosophy*, 3 (1983): 89–101. Translation of Martin Heidegger, *Hebel-der Hausfreund.* Pfullingen: Neske, 1957.

———. *Heraclitus. The Inception of Occidental Thinking and Logic: Heraclitus's Doctrine of the* Logos. Translated by Julia Goesser Assaiante and S. Montgomery Ewegen. London: Bloomsbury Academic, 2018. Translation of Martin Heidegger, *Gesamtausgabe*, Vol. 55, *Heraklit. Der Angang des abendländischen Denkens. Logik Heraklits Lehre vom Logos.* Edited by Manfred S. Frings. Frankfurt am Main: Klostermann, 1979, 2nd rev. ed. 1987; 3rd ed., 1994.

———. *Hölderlin's Hymns "Germania" and "The Rhein."* Translated by William McNeill and Julia Anne Ireland. Bloomington: Indiana University Press, 2014. Translation of Martin Heidegger, *Gesamtausgabe*, Vol. 39, *Hölderlins Hymnen "Germanien" und "Der Rhein."* Edited by Susanne Ziegler. Frankfurt am Main: Klostermann, 1980, 2nd rev. ed. 1989.

———. *Holzwege, Gesamtausgabe*, Vol. 5. Edited by Friedrich-Wilhelm v. Herrmann. Frankfurt am Main: Klostermann, 1950; 6th rev. ed. 1980.

———. *Logic as the Question Concerning the Essence of Language.* Translated by Wanda Torres Gregory and Yvonne Unna. Albany: State University of New York Press, 2010. Translation of Martin Heidegger, *Gesamtausgabe*, Vol. 38, *Logik als die Frage nach dem Wesen der Sprache.* Edited by Günter Seubold. Frankfurt am Main: Klostermann, 1998.

———. *On the Essence of Language. The Metaphysics of Language and the Essencing of the Word. Concerning Herder's Treatise* On the Origin of Language. Translated by Wanda Torres Gregory and Yvonne Unna. Albany, New York: State University of New York Press, 2004. Translation of Martin Heidegger, *Gesamtausgabe*, Vol. 85, *Vom Wesen der Sprache. Die Metaphysik der Sprache und die Wesung des Wortes. Zu Herders Abhandlung "Über den Ursprung der Sprache."* Edited by Ingrid Schüßler. Frankfurt am Main: Klostermann, 1999.

———. *On the Way to Language*. Translated by Peter D. Hertz. New York: Harper & Row, 1971. Translation of Martin Heidegger, *Unterwegs zur Sprache*. Stuttgart: Neske, 1959; 7th ed. 1982.

———. *Pathmarks*. Edited by William McNeill. Cambridge: Cambridge University Press, 1998. Translation of Martin Heidegger, *Gesamtausgabe*, Vol. 9, *Wegmarken*. Edited by Friedrich-Wilhelm von Herrmann. Frankfurt am Main: Klostermann, 1976.

———. *Poetry, Language, Thought*. Essays translated by Albert Hofstadter. New York: Harper & Row, 1971.

———. *Ponderings II–VI: Black Notebooks 1931-1938*. Translated by Richard Roczewicz. Bloomington: Indiana University Press, 2016. Translation of Martin Heidegger, *Gesamtausgabe*, Vol. 94, *Überlegungen II–VI (Schwarze Hefte 1931–1938)*. Edited by Peter Trawny. Frankfurt am Main: Klostermann, 2014.

———. *Ponderings VII–XII: Black Notebooks* 1938–1939. Translated by Richard Rojcewicz. Bloomington: Indiana University Press, 2017. Translation of Martin Heidegger, *Gesamtausgabe*, Vol. 94, *Überlegungen VII–XII (Schwarze Hefte 1938–1939)*. Edited by Peter Trawny. Frankfurt am Main: Klostermann, 2014.

———. *Ponderings XII-XV: Black Notebooks* 1939–1941. Translated by Richard Rojcewicz. Bloomington: Indiana University Press, 2017. Translation of Martin Heidegger, *Gesamtausgabe*, Vol. 94, *Überlegungen XII–XV (Schwarze Hefte 1939–1941)*. Edited by Peter Trawny. Frankfurt am Main: Klostermann, 2014.

———. *The Essence of Truth. On Plato's Cave Allegory and* Theaetetus. Translated by Ted Sadler. London: Continuum, 2002. Translation of Martin Heidegger, *Gesamtausgabe*, Vol. 34, *Vom Wesen der Wahrheit. Zu Platons Höhlengleichnis und Theätet*. Edited by Herrmann Mörchen. Frankfurt am Main: Klostermann, 1997.

———. *The Event*. Translated by Richard Rojcewicz. Bloomington: Indiana University Press, 2013. Translation of Martin Heidegger, *Gesamtausgabe*, Vol. 71, *Das Ereignis*. Edited by Friedrich-Wilhelm v. Herrmann. Frankfurt am Main: Klostermann, 2009.

———. *The Fundamental Concepts of Metaphysics: World, Finitude, Solitude*. Translated by William McNeill and Nicholas Walker. Bloomington: Indiana University Press, 1995. Translation of Martin Heidegger, *Gesamtausgabe*, Vol. 29/30, *Die Grundbegriffe der Metaphysik: Welt, Endlichkeit, Einsamkeit*. Edited by Friedrich-Wilhelm von Herrmann. Frankfurt am Main: Klostermann, 1983.

———. *The History of Beyng*. Translated by William McNeill and Jeffrey Powell. Bloomington, Indiana: Indiana University Press, 2015. Translation of Martin Heidegger, *Gesamtausgabe*, Vol. 69, *Die Geschichte des Seyns*. Edited by Peter Trawny. Frankfurt am Main: Klostermann, 1998; 2012.

———. *The Piety of Thinking*. Translated by J. G. Hart and J. C. Maraldo. Bloomington: Indiana University Press, 1976. Translation of Martin Heidegger, *Phänomenologie und Theologie*. Frankfurt am Main: Klostermann, 1970.

———. *The Principle of Reason*. Translated by Reginald Lilly. Bloomington: Indiana University Press, 1996. Translation of Martin Heidegger, *Der Satz vom Grund*. Stuttgart: Neske, 1957; 8th ed. 1997.

———. "The Self-Assertion of the German University." In *Martin Heidegger and National Socialism*. Edited by Gunther Neske and Emil Kettering. New York: Paragon House, 1990. Translation of Martin Heidegger, "Die Selbstbehauptung der deutschen Universität." Breslau: Korn, 1933.

———. "Traditional Language and Technological Language." Translated by Wanda Torres Gregory. *Journal of Philosophical Research*, vol. XXIII, 1998: 129–145. Translation of Martin Heidegger, *Überlieferte Sprache und Technische Sprache*. St. Gallen: Erker, 1989.

———. *Vorträge und Aufsätze*, *Gesamtausgabe*, Vol. 7. Edited by Friedrich-Wilhelm v. Herrmann. Frankfurt am Main: Klostermann, 2000.

———. *Was Heisst Denken?*, *Gesamtausgabe*, Vol. 8. Edited by Paola-Ludovika Coriando. Frankfurt am Main: Klostermann, 2002.

———. *Wegmarken*, *Gesamtausgabe*, Vol. 9. Edited by Friedrich-Wilhelm v. Herrmann. Frankfurt am Main: Klostermann, 2004.

———. *What is Called Thinking?* Translated by J. Glenn Gray. New York: Harper and Row, 1968. Translation of Martin Heidegger, *Was Heisst Denken?*, *Gesamtausgabe*, Vol. 8.

———. *Zum Wesen der Sprache und Zur Frage nach der Kunst*, *Gesamtausgabe*, Vol. 74. Edited by Thomas Regehly. Frankfurt am Main: Klostermann, 2011.

Heidegger, Martin and Eugen Fink. *Heraclitus Seminar*, *Gesamtausgabe*, Vol. 15. Translated by Charles H. Seiber. Evanston: Northwestern University Press, 1994. Translation of Martin Heidegger and Eugen Fink, *Heraklit*. Edited by Friedrich Wilhelm v. Herrmann. Frankfurt am Main: Klostermann, 2014.

Herder, Johann Gottfried. "Essay on the Origin of Language." In *On the Origin of Language. Two Essays by Jean-Jacques Rousseau and Johann Gottfried Herder*. Translated by Alexander Gode. New York: Frederick Ungar Publishing Company, 1966.

Idhe, Don. *Listening and Voice: Phenomenologies of Silence*. New York: State University of New York Press, 2nd ed. 2007.

Irigaray, Luce. "To Conceive Silence." In *To be Two*. Translated by Monique M. Rhodes and Marco F. Cocito-Monoc. New York: Routledge, 2001.

Keane, Niall. "The Silence of the Origin: Philosophy in Transition and the Essence of Thinking." In *Research in Phenomenology*, 43 (2013): 27–48.

Knowles, Adam. *Heidegger's Fascist Affinities: A Politics of Silence*. Stanford: Stanford University Press, 2019.

Lang, Berel. *Heidegger's Silence*. Ithaca and London: Cornell University Press, 1996.

May, Reinhard. *Heidegger's Hidden Sources*. Translated by Graham Parks. New York: Routledge, 1989.

Norwell Smith, David. *Sounding/Silence. Martin Heidegger at the Limits of Poetics*. New York: Fordham University Press, 2013.

Picard, Max. *The World of Silence*. Translated by Stanley Godwin. Wichita: Eighth Day Press, 2002.

Torres Gregory, Wanda. *Heidegger's Path to Language*. Lanham: Lexington Books, 2016.

Van Elferen, I., & Raeymaekers, S. "Silent Dark: The Orders of Silence." In *Journal for Cultural Research*, 19 (2015): 262–273.

Vallega-Neu, Daniela. "Heidegger's Reticence: From *Contributions* to *Das Ereignis* and toward *Gelassenheit*." In *Research in Phenomenology*, 45 (2015): 1–32.

Index

About the Author

Wanda Torres Gregory is Professor of philosophy at Simmons University, Boston. She is the author of *Heidegger's Path to Language* (Lanham, MD: Lexington Books, 2016), which has received positive reviews in *Notre Dame Philosophical Reviews* and *Comparative and Continental Philosophy.* Torres Gregory is also the co-translator of two of Heidegger's works: *Logic as the Question Concerning the Essence of Language* (New York, NY: SUNY Press, 2009), which was nominated for the Goethe Institute's 2010 Helen and Kurt Wolff Translator's Prize, and *On the Essence of Language. The Metaphysics of Language and the Essencing of the Word. Concerning Herder's Treatise On the Origin of Language* (New York, NY: SUNY Press, 2004), which was nominated for the American Translators' Association 2005 German Translation Award. In addition, she is the leading editor of the multicultural anthology in ethical theory *World Ethics* (Belmont, CA: Thomson-Wadsworth. 2003).

CPSIA information can be obtained
at www.ICGtesting.com
Printed in the USA
LVHW081810011122
732099LV00004B/179

9 781793 640031